THE NUMINOUS
COSMIC YEAR

YOUR ASTROLOGICAL ALMANAC

DISCOVER WHAT IS WRITTEN IN THE STARS

with Bess Matassa

aster

First published in Great Britain in 2021 by Aster, an imprint of Octopus Publishing Group Ltd, Carmelite House, 50 Victoria Embankment, London EC4Y 0DZ
www.octopusbooks.co.uk
www.octopusbooksusa.com

An Hachette UK Company
www.hachette.co.uk

Distributed in the US by Hachette Book Group, 1290 Avenue of the Americas, 4th and 5th Floors, New York, NY 10104

Distributed in Canada by Canadian Manda Group, 664 Annette St, Toronto, Ontario, Canada M6S 2C8

ISBN 978-1-78325-433-0

A CIP catalogue record for this book is available from the British Library.

Printed and bound in the UK.

10 9 8 7 6 5 4 3 2 1

Consultant Publisher: Kate Adams
Art Director: Jaz Bahra
Editor: Ella Parsons
Copyeditor: Alison Wormleighton
Designer: Megan van Staden
Assistant Production Managers: Lucy Carter + Nic Jones

Images: iStock, Shutterstock

This FSC® label means that materials used for the product have been responsibly sourced

MIX
Paper from responsible sources
FSC® C104740
www.fsc.org

CONTENTS

INTRODUCTION

You are already living in alignment with the stars. From the bold, beating-heart desires that course through your veins to the way you dress for the wild weather patterns that run through each month of the year, the wisdom of the cosmos is within you and all around you.

Have you ever stood up straighter and wiser to face the morning dawn in early January, ready to relish a reckoning with your life, a courageous confrontation that will test your solid-gold grit? You're already channelling Capricorn energy. Have you ever tumbled heart-first into the lush sparkle and shine of an endless August afternoon, with the feeling that the romance of the world is yours for the squeezing? That's the gorgeous glow of both the universal and your personal inner Leo.

Just as the Sun shifts into a different zodiac sign each month, amid all sorts of other planetary shuffles, so we experience – and try on for size – the 'feeling tone' of each sign. In other words, the collective emotional 'climate' created by particular cosmic energies. Regardless of what we know as our personal 'Star sign' (more on these soon), we all get to explore the properties symbolized by each month's astrological energies, as we gather new resources for our own life journeys.

Whichever hemisphere you live in, and whatever your sign, each of the 12 zodiac signs, along with their accompanying monthly energies, gifts us a new set of intention-setting principles and potentialities. As you set out into the as-yet-unknown territory of 2022, *The Numinous Cosmic Year* will light the way. A guide to both the shifting astrological currents and the influence of the celestial bodies on our daily lives, it will map your path forwards and within.

WHAT IS NUMINOUS ASTROLOGY?

The word 'numinous' refers to that which is unknowable, mysterious and holy, and it connects us with the parts of our ethereal experience on Earth that simply can't be 'proven'. You perceive it through your instincts and visions, and in your sleeping and waking dreams. The numinous is in the ineffable, inexplicable, intuitive stardust that animates everything we cannot see.

While we sometimes seek to understand astrology through the technical lines and degrees on a birth chart, or by scientific measures like the pull of the Moon on Earth's monthly tides, this dynamic, living language of signs and symbols is actually accessible to us all *right now*. An intuitive practice for describing the mysteries of life itself, astrology sits in the liminal space (an area of transition) somewhere between art and psychology, a ticket straight into the heart of life's big 'whys'.

With 2,000-year-old roots in ancient Babylon and the eastern Mediterranean, astrology has long been inspiring humans to look to the sky to make sense of who we are and what we are experiencing. The ancient Greek physician Hippocrates stated: 'A physician without a knowledge of astrology has no right to call himself a physician.' And among the myriad schools and approaches to astrology, the 12 zodiac signs and the planetary archetypes are described with startling similarity – even between civilizations that would have had no 'technical' way to communicate this information to one another. The language of astrology is truly universal, speaking to our fundamental human desires, challenges, gifts and visions.

Numinous Astrology is descended directly from the New Age revival of the 1960s and 1970s. Rather than a predictive, deterministic tool that tells us what's going to happen to us, astrology becomes a living language – a mystical meaning-maker that brings us into a tango with the interwoven principles of fate and free will. If we're willing to investigate what really makes us tick, we can use astrology to wake us up to the reciprocal relationship between what's 'out there' and what's 'in here'.

Building on this more evolutionary, human approach and updating it for the 'Now Age', Numinous Astrology adds some bedazzling jewels and pop rock beats to the celestial equation. Instead of having to get high and holy on a mountain (although if that's your jam, by all means go for it!), it's about starting exactly where you are, with what you hold in your hands today. Want to learn about Taurus energy? Watch a rose slowly open its petals or let a rich, dark chocolate bar melt in your mouth. Curious about what makes Sagittarius tick? Roll down the windows in your car, letting the wind tousle your locks and the road rise to meet you.

Each of the 12 seasons presented in this almanac, along with the monthly planetary transits that are unique to the year ahead, creates a lifeworld. This is your individual world of experiences, made to be touched, tasted and investigated. And each month, we'll invite you to explore these energies in tangible ways, through everything from journal prompts to style tips. When we come closer to the lived expression of these signs' energies in the world, we come closer to how they live inside each of us – encouraging us to explore our own numinous natures and celebrate the biodiversity within us.

NOTES ON USING THIS COSMIC YEAR ALMANAC

TWO WAYS TO USE THIS BOOK

A guide to the 'feeling tone' of each astrological season

Regardless of your personal astrology (as depicted in your individual birth chart), each month gives you the chance to try on the 'feeling tones' – the ideas, looks, scents and sounds – of the astrological archetypes it contains.

As such, you can treat this almanac as a cosmic dressing-up box, zipping into the energies that are outlined and trying them on for size.

A personalized journey for your Sun, Moon and Rising signs

Each month, the Sun moves into a different zodiac sign – this is what gives each of us our Star sign or Sun sign, based on our date of birth. Beyond this Sun sign, we each have an entire birth chart – a love letter to us personally penned by the cosmos – that shows the position of all the planets at the moment we arrived on Planet Earth.

You can find plenty of places online to enter your birth details (time, date and place) and quickly pull up your chart (and our *Numinous Astro Deck* is a complete system for learning how to interpret it).

As a quick way to dive in, looking to your Sun, Moon and Rising signs reveals the signature that anchors your birth chart, a shorthand to the liveable, breathable story of *you*!

Your Sun sign sits at the centre of it all – the hero you already are and are always becoming.

Your Moon sign reveals what you need in order to feel safe on a soul level – your backpack of nourishing treats to stock up on for the ride.

And your Rising sign is a powerful point of alchemy between the two, catalysing your growth by leading you towards greater self-awareness and more authentic self-expression.

Each of the 12 signs has something to learn from the others, and the sign-by-sign invitations in this almanac offer personalized astral navigation tips.

Depending on where you find yourself and what you need most, you might choose to read for your Sun sign, Moon sign, Rising sign or all three.

☉ YOUR SUN SIGN: *The Mission* – individuating function

This sign symbolizes a dynamic, heroic mission that unfolds over the course of your lifetime. For example, you aren't simply 'an Aquarius' with a list of traits that are given and fixed. Instead, you're on an 'Aquarius solar mission', to explore the archetypal ways of being and to develop the qualities that Aquarius represents.

✦ Read for your Sun sign: Do this when you are ready to sparkle and shine in a given month and are seeking to reconnect to your individuality and purpose.

☽ YOUR MOON SIGN: *The Locket* – sheltering function

This sign in your chart holds the keys to your private inner sanctum. The source of both your sensitized sustenance and your innate emotional response, it reveals the quality of your sensitivity. Connecting with its energy shows what you need in order to feel safe and nourished, so you can head out into the world to complete your Sun sign mission.

✦ Read for your Moon sign: Do this when you are craving a connection with your inner nature and are ready to support yourself from the inside out with a dose of soulful nourishment.

↑↑↑ YOUR RISING SIGN: *The Mirror* – **reflective function**

Affecting both how you meet life and how life meets you, your Rising sign maps out the terrain of your personal journey: the ways in which you express your Sun sign mission, the kinds of themes and situations that will draw you closer to yourself, and the qualities you are being challenged to 'take on'.

✦ Read for your Rising sign: Do this when you feel poised to begin anew in a particular month and are ready to shake off the death throes of an old cycle or identity.

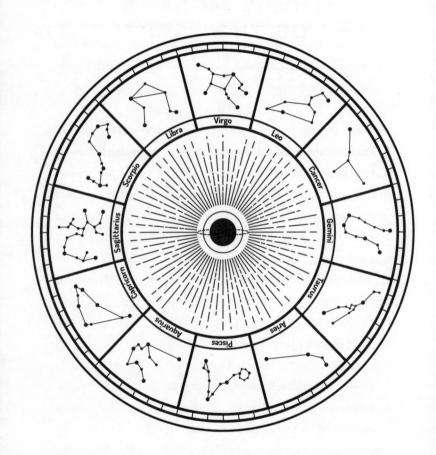

THE 12 ZODIAC SIGNS +
THE 12 MONTHS
OF THE YEAR

S tudying the personal configurations and concentrations of our birth charts offers a complex understanding of ourselves and our particular path through the world. But our shared journey through the year offers every one of us the opportunity to harness the potent energies symbolized by each month's primary sign archetype.

The dates the Sun spends in each sign don't exactly sync with the dates of each calendar month, but the sign in which we 'enter' the month can be thought of as its dominant energy – for example, we enter January while the Sun is in Capricorn, so this sign describes the dominant feeling tone of the month.

As we travel through the wheel of the year, we invite you to play with the principles described here, slipping into each of the sign energies and their teachings and getting curious about which feel scratchier and which seem to fit you like a second skin. No matter which hemisphere we live in, each season of the year contains a holy trinity of zodiac sign energies that ask us to honour a certain cycle of development and awareness within ourselves. Make connecting with these energies a conscious practice as the years go by, and you will begin to develop a deeper awareness of, and sense of connection to, the cycles of your life.

JANUARY/FEBRUARY/MARCH

The trinity of sign energies associated with the 'technical' start of the calendar year is actually a potent astral moment of culmination, as the cosmic calendar stands poised to begin anew in late March. These three 'final' signs of the zodiac – Capricorn, Aquarius and Pisces – ask us to fortify trust in our self-sufficient legacy, so we can find the grit to push past the finish line and the focus to tie up loose ends before we relax into the divine inspiration that will ignite our next adventure.

♑ JANUARY // Capricorn: *The gift of ownership*

January's energy is sovereign and mature, asking us to consolidate and weatherproof our ambitions for the long haul. This means owning up to our limitations and drawing deep from our hard-won wisdom. It's the season for fortifying rock-solid foundations, testing our mettle and birthing beautifully self-governed boundaries.

♒ FEBRUARY // Aquarius: *The gift of vision*

February's energy is prophetic and unfettered, asking us to untangle ourselves from past patterning in favour of revolutionary thinking that takes us far beyond the roads we know. It's the season for adopting broader and bolder perspectives, finding the beauty in groundlessness and no longer clinging to the 'way it is'.

♓ MARCH // Pisces: *The gift of release*

March's energies are immersive and evanescent, asking us to melt into our environment without prejudice and to practise the fine art of becoming 'invisible' – softening any hard internal edges and allowing ourselves to fuse with whatever feelings arise. It's the season for letting go and submitting to our status as sparkling specks amid a dazzling sea of stars.

APRIL/MAY/JUNE

The astrological year 'begins' in late March when the Sun enters Aries, the first sign of the zodiac, and this seasonal trinity of signs is infused with newness and exhilarating emergence. Aries, Taurus and Gemini ask us to make like baby chicks or sprouting blades of grass, pushing ourselves over the endlessly self-generating starting line and summoning the boldness to begin again and again and again.

♈ APRIL // Aries: *The gift of arrival*

April's energy is lean and focused, asking us to streamline and invigorate our lives, reducing them to essentials as we burn ourselves 'clean' of any excess baggage and move forwards unencumbered as our one-and-only selves. It's the season to rev your engine, have some fun with fire-starting friction and delight in your capacity to make a dent in the earth.

♉ MAY // Taurus: *The gift of worthiness*

May's energy is rich and fertile, asking us to plump up and root down, banishing scarcity mentality and bolstering our belief in life's endless buffet as we allow ourselves to reach for whatever just feels good. It's the season for feeding your inner fullness, connecting to the senses and valuing yourself as more than just 'good enough'.

♊ JUNE // Gemini: *The gift of curiosity*

June's energy is multi-faceted and winged, asking us to shape-shift and sample the world tapas-style, hollowing our creative channels to pick up inspiration on the go. It's the season for mixing, matching and being bedazzled by the rainbow of possible pollination stations, while finding breath in the spaces in between.

JULY / AUGUST / SEPTEMBER

Our third trinity of seasonal energies, governed by Cancer, Leo and Virgo, is all about sweet, supple self-expression and tender nurturing, as we get cosy with our inner self, dive into our luscious creative juices and divine the precise contours of our precious nature.

♋ JULY // Cancer: *The gift of belonging*

July's energy encircles and incubates us, asking us to seek shelter in our secret diaries and rhythmically dilate and contract to bring big feelings down the birthing canal. It's the season for tucking in, exploring our lineage, finding what feels like home and getting friendly with our innate sensitivity.

♌ AUGUST // Leo: *The gift of simplicity*

August's energy is shiny and precious, asking us to see and be seen through the eyes of love, trusting in the straightforward ardour of the heart. It's the season for penning larger-than-life personal mythologies, taking a chance on sweet romance and remembering our rightful role as the creator of our own existence.

♍ SEPTEMBER // Virgo: *The gift of integrity*

September's energy is sentient and integral, asking us to bow down, commit and assess the subtlest environmental feedback as we fine-tune a bespoke holistic responsiveness. It's the season for divining precisely where you want to place your power and devotion, and for recalibrating your intricate energy needs.

OCTOBER/NOVEMBER/DECEMBER

Our final trinity of the year, guided by Libra, Scorpio and Sagittarius, asks us to step up and out beyond ourselves and meet the world that faces us – whether this means grappling with the needs and desires of our fellow human beings or coming head to head with the forces of evolutionary change.

♎ OCTOBER // Libra: *The gift of relating*

October's energy is aspirational and aligned, asking us to first embrace exactly what is present in our lives so that we can assess and perfect our path. It's the season for considering cause and effect, balancing personal willpower with partnered compromise, and deciding exactly what's right for you, right now.

♏ NOVEMBER // Scorpio: *The gift of desire*

November's energy is penetrating and excavating, asking us to dive beneath and scour our inner workings, divining which pieces of ourselves are eternal and unbreakable, and being willing to compost the rest. It's the season for getting good with our ghosts, as we slough off shame and strip down to the naked intimacy of our sheer desires.

♐ DECEMBER // Sagittarius: *The gift of seeking*

December's energy is kinetic and untameable, asking us to throw open the metaphorical windows, stretch our muscles and move beyond constrictive containments. It's the season for adventurously seeking and expanding our capacity for risk, with the faith that our own life is on our side.

GALACTIC GLOSSARY

Use these key terms to help you navigate the astral realm this year.

THE PLANETS

From the primal desire for intimacy to the necessity of undergoing psychological deaths and rebirths, every planet in the heavens represents one of our innate human urges. Each one of the celestial bodies listed here moves through the 12 signs at different rates (with the close-to-home Moon shifting zodiac signs every two and a half days, while far-out planet Neptune takes fourteen years to change signs). These movements not only create our personal birth chart – which shows the planets placed in different signs at our specific moment of entry into the world – they also represent collective energies we can harness throughout any given year, no matter what is in our chart.

You can think of each planet as a particular dish, and the sign it moves through as giving it a certain seasoning or flavour. For example, the pleasure principle of Venus will taste much more piquant as it travels through hot-blooded Aries than it will in ethereal Pisces, bringing passions to the surface and helping us boldly claim our desires.

☉ ☽ The luminaries (Sun/Moon/Rising)

THE BEING PRINCIPLE - WHO WE ARE: Consisting of the cosmic forces held closest to our chest, this trinity connects us to our essence – our individual mission (Sun), soul nourishment (Moon) and adventurous encounters with the wider world (Rising).

☿ ♀ ♂ The personal planets (Mercury/Venus/Mars)

THE DOING PRINCIPLE - HOW WE MOVE: These planets describe the ins and outs of life on the ground: processing and metabolizing life (Mercury), receiving and savouring life (Venus) and empowering our life force to make things happen (Mars).

♃ ♄ ⚷ The transpersonal planets (Jupiter/Saturn) + Chiron

THE GROWTH PRINCIPLE - HOW WE REACH: This trio reveals our cosmic curriculum. Each shows a different style of study: expansion through self-trust (Jupiter), maturity through self-sufficiency (Saturn) and healing through self-acceptance (Chiron – a planetoid and comet that orbits between Saturn and Uranus, symbolically experienced as touchy-feely terrain that's ripe for extra tenderness).

♅ ♆ ♀ The outer planets (Uranus/Neptune/Pluto)

THE EVOLUTION PRINCIPLE - WHAT MOVES US: Far out from Earth, these planets ask us to evolve on a massive scale: reorienting and shocking us towards new life (Uranus), releasing and going 'beyond' life (Neptune) and excavating and uprooting old life (Pluto).

THE NORTH NODE

A power point that connects the Sun, Moon and Earth, the North Node exerts a magnetic pull that keeps us honest about our commitment to evolve. Urging us towards a big-picture purpose, its energy helps us align with the glimmer of our higher self.

RETROGRADES

Occurring when a planet seems to slow down and move 'backwards', retrogrades (Rx) are no cause for alarm. In fact, the notorious Mercury retrograde cycle occurs up to four times per year, and most of the outer planets spend up to half the year moving in 'reverse'. The planetary slumber parties of the cosmos, retrograde cycles simply offer us an intimate, between-the-sheets encounter with the planet in question, letting us swap a more external engagement with its energies for an internal investigation. As a planet then 'stations direct', it prepares to head forwards once again. At this point, we're invited to hit the streets and take action, armed with a more complex inner knowledge of this celestial body.

ASPECTS

Aspects describe how different sign energies interact, both challenging and supporting one another to grow and evolve.

Conjunction

THE MISSION STATEMENT: Two of the same signs amplify and empower one another (for example Pisces and Pisces).

Inconjunct or Quincunx

THE HIDDEN MESSAGE: Signs in different elements and modalities ask for radical acceptance of each other's complexities (for example Cardinal Earth Capricorn and Fixed Fire Leo).

Opposition or Polarity

THE IMPASSIONED DEBATE: Planets in opposing signs provide contrast for and seek to equilibrate one another (for example Fixed Earth Taurus and Fixed Water Scorpio).

Sextile

EXTRASENSORY PERCEPTION: Signs of compatible elements experiment with and expand one another (for example Air and Fire signs, or Earth and Water signs).

Semi-sextile

THE PEP TALK: Neighbouring signs learn to adjust to and support one another (for example the sixth sign of Virgo and the seventh sign of Libra).

Square

THE CONSTRUCTIVE DIALOGUE: Signs with the same modality but differing elements challenge and motivate one another (for example Fixed Air Aquarius and Fixed Earth Taurus).

Trine

THE HEART-TO-HEART: Signs of the same element flow together and enjoy one another (for example Fire signs Aries and Sagittarius).

THIS YEAR'S RETROGRADE CYCLES

Use this guide to align with and enjoy the retrograde slow jams.

Mercury retrograde (14 January–4 February; 10 May–3 June; 10 September–2 October)

THE SUBPLOT: The footnotes and hidden metaphors to our life story, Mercury Rx asks us to refine our beliefs and perceptions.

Venus retrograde (19 December 2021– 29 January 2022)

THE SLOW DANCE: A tantalizing tango with everything we hold close to our hearts, Venus Rx asks us to refine what we love and how we love it.

♂

Mars retrograde (30 October 2022–12 January 2023)

THE PIT STOP: A chance to press pause on endless go-getting and to replenish our reserves, Mars Rx asks us to refine how we use our life-force fuel.

♃

Jupiter retrograde (28 July–23 November)

THE HOLDING PATTERN: Like an extra spin round the airport before landing, Jupiter Rx asks us to refine our grand plans and wild expansions.

♄

Saturn retrograde (4 June–23 October)

THE MARATHON: A slow-burn strengthener of our wise maturity, Saturn Rx asks us to refine our definitions of success and effort.

Uranus retrograde (20 August 2021–18 January 2022; 24 August 2022–22 January 2023)

THE INNER SHIFT: An electrically charged opportunity to catalyse shifts from the inside out, Uranus Rx asks us to refine our relationship to change and creative revolution.

Neptune retrograde (28 June–4 December)

THE FANTASY SUITE: A chance to check in with our highest hopes, Neptune Rx asks us to refine our understanding of happiness and bring our dreams down to earth.

Pluto retrograde (29 April–8 October)

THE FUNERAL PYRE: An evolutionary call to align our personal power with the powers that be, Pluto Rx asks us to refine our willingness to excavate the old and rise again renewed.

A NOTE ON 2022: BUOYANCY + BREATH WORK

The energy of 2022 is akin to a busy city intersection. We are invited to consider where we place our attention, get curious about shifting perspectives and leave some openings in our lives for the Divine to slip inside. This year's Mercury retrograde cycles in Air signs ask us to become little astral antennae – noticing the nearly invisible synchronicities that surround us and channelling new intel so we can revise the parts of our stories that have begun to stifle us. Jupiter's final tour through Pisces and shift into Aries marks an opportunity to let our soul's growth feel 'the right size' as we learn to naturally assert ourselves in a way that's neither forced nor apologetic. And Saturn's final full year in Aquarius invites us to radically accept all our oddball tendencies, seeing even the strangest parts of ourselves as an opportunity to master our particular form of magic. To top it all off, we are in a '6 year' (the sum of the digits in the year: $2 + 0 + 2 + 2 = 6$), symbolized in the Tarot by The Lovers card. Ruled by the sign of Gemini, The Lovers card invites us to consider both affect (the outward expression of our emotions) and effect, remembering that our impact is felt even when we can't see the results, and that what we long for out in the world also longs to love us back. All in all, it's a year to remain nimble and adaptable, as we attune to balancing our uptake with our output, and agree to meet whatever leads us on the dance floor with a willingness to shimmy and shape-shift.

WORKING WITH
THE ELEMENTS

Each of the 12 months and associated signs is marked by an element, which reveals its basic 'charge'. The energetic building blocks of the astrological year, the elements help us check in with the feeling tone of each season.

Each of the four elements speaks to a core set of values and ways of being in the world. If you want to embody and explore these, you don't have to go very far at all! Turn the oven on and watch Fire energy warm your dinner. Open the tap to run a bath and witness how Water pulls you down and into the tub. Watch clouds rushing past or the shifting angle of light on a wall and engage Air's changeable perspective. Simply become aware of your body and the gravity keeping your feet on the ground to be reminded of the enduring stability of Earth.

Use the four elements to take a 'temperature check' of the month.

The Earth months (January/May/September; Capricorn/Taurus/Virgo)

SENSING FUNCTION - THE VALUE OF EMBODIMENT: Resources. Rhythm. Tangibility. The Earth element invites us into the realm of the physical senses. Touching their toes to the ground and reading environmental rhythms, each Earth month asks us to touch base with the material 'realities' of the world, by treasuring that which we can see, touch, taste and smell, and developing our sense of worth, competence and contribution.

The Air months (February/June/October; Aquarius/Gemini/Libra)

THINKING FUNCTION - THE VALUE OF COMPREHENSION: Vision. Ideals. Exchange. The Air element invites us into the realm of mental concepts. Opening wide to the shifting breezes and electrical currents of change, each Air month wants us to draw connections, understand the 'how' of things and play with the presence of what we perceive, so we can unlock stuck beliefs and glimpse future visions of what might be possible.

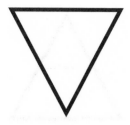

The Water months (March/July/November; Pisces/Cancer/Scorpio)

FEELING FUNCTION – THE VALUE OF CLOSENESS: Longing. Lovability. Memory. Water invites us into the realm of private emotions. Sheltering the lair of our inner longings, each Water month asks us to travel into the hidden coves of our psyches. As we come into intimacy with the unseen parts of ourselves, we expand our capacity for empathy and develop a sweetness towards these secret lives that sends us tumbling into one another's arms.

The Fire months (April/August/December; Aries/Leo/Sagittarius)

INTUITING FUNCTION – THE VALUE OF SIGNIFICANCE: Passion. Vitality. Creation. Fire invites us into the realm of spirit. Coming 'out of nowhere', each Fire month asks us to assess and connect to our personal and intuitive significance: the sense that our individual existence is both meaningful and potent, and that our creative urges serve to help us uncover the larger-than-life 'why' of our lives.

MODALITIES

In addition to the four elements, which give each sign a particular 'charge', the 12 signs are also separated into three modes of expression known as 'modalities', which represent magic modes of moving through the world.

♈ ♋ ♎ ♑

The Cardinal signs (Aries/Cancer/Libra/Capricorn)

These signs initiate their respective seasons on the yearly equinoxes and solstices, powering up and pointing the way.

♉ ♌ ♏ ♒

The Fixed signs (Taurus/Leo/Scorpio/Aquarius)

These signs stabilize and 'steep' us in the central month of a season, tapping into founts of inner force.

♊ ♍ ♐ ♓

The Mutable signs (Gemini/Virgo/Sagittarius/Pisces)

Marking the end of each season, these are here to help us adjust and adapt to life's changing weather patterns.

FLOWING WITH THE
LUNAR CYCLES

Each month, the Moon charts a curvaceous course through each of the 12 signs, shifting sign energies about every two and a half days. During this journey, it presents different facets and feeling tones, from the all-but-a-glimmer New Moon to the fertile and fat Full Moon, and back again. Connecting with the lunar cycles syncs us with our shifting sensations, and understanding each phase can help us calibrate our inner rhythms.

◯ NEW MOON PHASE

The New Moon phase is our return to innocence, no matter what hard knocks have come before. It invites us to attend to what is beginning to glimmer and pop up in our lives, so use this time to plant an interstellar seed without worrying about outcomes.

◖ WAXING MOON PHASE

Just like a shiny, shampooed convertible, the Waxing Moon calls on your buffing and polishing skills for the ride ahead. Treat this phase like a sweetly sweaty workout session, flexing the muscle of your life force to make your hopes and dreams real and road-ready.

 FULL MOON PHASE

A potent moment of emotional party-going, the Full Moon marks the 'most' of something in our lives. A celebratory call to feast on what is ripened and fully grown, this phase asks us to acknowledge what is coming to culmination and to celebrate just how far we've come.

WANING MOON PHASE

The lunar outbreath of the month, the Waning Moon phase is a time for laying our bodies down and simply letting the sensations wash over us without having to adjust. A profound moment of making peace with reality, this phase invites us to allow and accept, as we loosen our grip and let go.

Refer back to these pages as you engage with the teachings and invitations of each month – but may your own numinous nature be your guide as you traverse the astrological seasons of the year. And know that each time you encounter words like 'goddess', 'spirit', and 'divine', the definition of these deities is yours alone – as lovingly limitless as the worlds within you and the stars above you.

MONDAY	TUESDAY	WEDNESDAY	THURSDAY	FRIDAY	SATURDAY	SUNDAY
						2 JANUARY New Moon in Capricorn Mercury enters Aquarius
				14 JANUARY Mercury stations retrograde in Aquarius		
17 JANUARY Full Moon in Cancer	**18 JANUARY** Uranus stations direct in Taurus + the North Node enters Taurus		**20 JANUARY** Sun enters Aquarius			
24 JANUARY Mars enters Capricorn					**29 JANUARY** Venus stations direct in Capricorn	

JANUARY

CLAIM YOUR CASTLE

CLAIM YOUR CASTLE

January's astrology wants you to begin with your beautiful bones. To sink, stately and sovereign, into the shape of your body and your life, exactly as they are. To acknowledge all your capacities and constraints; your longings and limits. And to know that you have every right to be right here – wherever 'here' is.

While we sometimes think of January as a brand new baby chick beginning in the cosmos – our annual opportunity to wipe the decks crystal clear and simply start over – it also brings us to a culmination point, marked by the tenth sign, Capricorn. The ancient arbiter of time itself, Capricorn energy invites us to consider both infinite timelessness and the boundaries of our finite incarnation, as well as what legacy we will leave with this one-life-only body.

In the Tarot, January is governed by the firm hand of Capricorn's ruling card, The Devil. Forget any 'sinful' notions of a punitive universe this may conjure up! This card actually denotes a decadent, entirely self-dedicated opportunity to break free of whatever binds us – asking us to cut the cords on spin cycles of shame and self-recrimination. The Devil invites us to strike a power pose from the inside out, as we exercise our inner authority and focus on where to start calling the shots.

Instead of hasty 'New Year, new me' resolutions, this month is actually a time to summon up the self-possessed majesty of your accumulated experience on this planet and to take a long, luxurious look at your lineage. January asks us to trust in our own dominion. Where in your life can you stake a claim to what you actually already own? And what is asking to be integrated before you brave the elements once again?

Before you think about starting over, you are invited to settle into your skin and consider how far you've come. Let this month be your after-dinner leather armchair, holding you as you warm yourself at a hearth fired up with the tree trunks you've grown and chopped with your own two hands.

And while we can't always get what we want, January reminds us that the things worth wanting are worth both waiting and working for. This month's alpine survival school energy reveals that striving and stickability can be just as satisfying as any arrival, and that there is a crystal-cut diamond encased within the ice castle of every hardship.

JANUARY DATES WITH DESTINY:
YOUR PRECIOUS POWER PACK

With a Mercury retrograde journey kicking off this January (the first of three in 2022 that are all in Air signs), coupled with pleasure-pumping Venus travelling retrograde through earthbound Capricorn, **this month asks us to attend to our energy portals – examining how and what we take in and put out, and what we're available to receive.**

Take this month to consider your concepts of success and achievement. When you're working towards a goal, what feeds the foundation of your operation? How do you 'fill up' to fuel forwards? And what does it feel like to get on top of it? When you've reached a perceived pinnacle, are you able to rest in the ski lodge and pour the hot cocoa, or do you immediately start flexing towards the next peak? January wants you to rewrite your tales of triumph, treating every moment like a miniature gold medal that can never be melted down.

New Moon in Capricorn

RUGGED + REGAL: New Moons are itty-bitty buds of potential on the distant horizon, inviting us to see what might sprout from nearly invisible intentions. This emergent Capricorn New Moon asks us to consider our borders, our boundaries and the shape of our lives: what holds us, what we hold fast to and what we can't hold any more. Take this time to **commit to creating clearer containers**, treating this Moon like a climbing rose or a haiku, where pruning brings on a greater bounty.

Mercury enters Aquarius

COOL IT DOWN: The cosmic nervous system that allows us to process this wild world, Mercury governs our perceptions, projections, filters and feedback loops – how we take up information from our environment, form our thoughts and express them verbally, and also how we 'metabolize' experience more broadly, swallowing our life experiences into our bodies and deciding which bits to digest as vital energy. With Mercury's entry into Aquarius, we're asked to cool it down – exercising deep discernment without getting stuck in the messy machinations of sentimentality. Take this time to **notice how your whole self perceives and reacts to change.** Does your pulse quicken? Does your mouth go dry? Do you root down and rail against it, or wave your hands towards the sky with glee?

Rather than flying off the handle as some new piece of intel threatens to upend your rooted belief systems, consider your interior landscape as an evolving biosphere and let different trees and flowers inside you come alive in this shifting weather.

Mercury stations retrograde in Aquarius
(enters Capricorn on 26th; stations direct in Capricorn on 4 February)

THE VISTA POINT: Any planetary retrograde brings the energy of an after-school sleepover – a chance to take it home after hours and get to know what really makes it tick. Each Mercury retrograde is an opportunity to process your perceived experience of the world. During this cycle, you get to keep whichever parts of each storyline or experience strengthen you, and flush out those that are ready for editing. In Aquarius, this editing process quickens and aerates, asking us to regard our life from a higher vista point. Use your cosmic binoculars and **notice where you are deep in the wild weeds with a situation or relationship, as you see things from a fresh perspective**. After Mercury moves into Capricorn on the 26th, consider what an older, wiser you would say, years from now.

Full Moon in Cancer

A FEAST OF FEELINGS: Full Moons are feasts of megawatt illumination, inviting us to see it all, bless it all and join the conga line on the dance floor. Like a ripe avocado or a scoop of cashew-milk ice cream, the Cancer Full Moon offers us an opportunity to indulge in the 'good' fat of our feelings. **Consider where your full body is asking you to feel something.** Maybe it's anger. Or jealousy. Or joy. No matter the tone or texture, this is a Moon meant for letting it grow large inside of you without fear. Care for it like a treasured house guest, tucking it into bed with a warm mug of tea and a smooch.

Uranus stations direct in Taurus
(retrograde since 20 August 2021)
+ the North Node enters Taurus

SHIFTING SOURCES OF SUSTENANCE: Part of the trinity of outer planets (Uranus, Neptune, Pluto) that initiates us into soul-centric surrender, Uranus accelerates our evolutionary metabolism for change. We're almost at the halfway point of Uranus' seven-year journey through Taurus. And as its forward motion resumes (when planets go retrograde, they appear to be moving backwards and ask for more inward-facing consideration) and is joined in

Taurus by the North Node (an astral point that connects us to our big-picture purpose), it's time to revise our evolutionary in-flight meal plan. What will sustain you on your trajectory right now? And **how are you balancing your material security with giving your soul what it needs?** Where are you willing to risk temporary 'discomfort' for a more permanent sense of pleasure?

Sun enters Aquarius

READY FOR OFF-ROADING: Each of the Sun's monthly transitions between signs builds upon the energy of its predecessor and also opens us towards a new orientation. Aquarius enters the mix to reveal to us what exactly we've been striving for, along with an end point that has been but a pinprick in our awareness until now. This readies us for a radical dismantling of Capricorn's legacy-building and turf-claiming. In the midst of this transition, ask yourself: **What have I mastered that needs no more mustering?** And what new ideas and inspiration are calling me towards a fresh path?

Mars enters Capricorn

WORK IT FOR WHAT'S WORTH IT: Mars is our empowered inner engine, driving us to go after what we want with a hunger honed by pure desire. Our petrol pump of action and life-force energy, it represents the power cable that connects us with our right to be here, to take up space and to come fiercely alive to our carnal imprint. Having been travelling through the wide-open world of dynamo Sagittarius since mid-December 2021, this shift into Capricorn focuses our energy, asking us to get down to the business of doing whatever we came here to do. It is time to **consider the long-haul effects of our actions** and think about exactly how we want to spread our precious seed.

Venus stations direct in Capricorn
(retrograde since 19 December 2021)

THE GOLD STANDARD: Representing our boudoir of receptivity, Venus energy urges us to dilate and magnetize, as we explore both how we attract and what we're attracted to. This libidinous love bunny reminds us that what we love in the world also wants to love us back: that the qualities we hold dear are also contained within us. With Venus in opulent, cave-aged Capricorn, we're asked to explore what we're available for and where we might be able to raise the bar on our sensual standards. Consider where you could **swap a temporary pleasure fix for a more lasting love**, looking at your desires and partnerships as an opportunity to see what's truly meant to make it 'til death do you part.

STAR PARTY:
NEW YEAR'S DAY (1 JANUARY)

While New Year's Day shifts across cultures, the Julian and Gregorian calendars fixed 1 January as the year's inaugural moment, connecting this month to the god Janus – lord of thresholds. Before you simply scream 'out with the old and in with the new', take a little time to honour the in-between. No matter how small or seemingly insignificant it is, consider where you're in transition right now and how you can meet yourself exactly where you are.

SIGN-BY-SIGN
GUIDE TO JANUARY

♑ CAPRICORN

It's your time, queenly climber! January invites you to settle in and look upon your kingdom from a secure position of creative competence. Notice the effort needed to ease into your existence right now – attending to the places that might merit a little more push as well as the spots that are calling you to sink serenely down into the groove of what's already been achieved. Your resilience and inner resources are unparalleled in the entire zodiac, and your birthday month asks you to find a regal rhythm that balances sweat with sweetness, knowing when it's time to lean back on your throne and simply enjoy it.

✦ With Venus shifting from retrograde to direct in your sign this month, the spotlight is on how you're able to let yourself be loved. Explore all of your efforts to 'hold up' life and keep it running smoothly for those around you, and look at how some of those efforts could be distracting you from your own personal need for support. If you are the one who's usually packing the lunches and checking the oil, see where in your life you could reach out to be lifted up right now. It's okay to be the one being held for once.

♒ AQUARIUS

Concerned with the creation (and destruction) of structures and systems, both Aquarius and Capricorn are fit to take over the world. January is your chance to land your experimental visions on solid ground and to carefully consider the deeper roots and motivations beneath your empire-building hustle.

✦ With the year's first Mercury retrograde transiting your sign, use this month to consider how all the moving parts of your life vibrate in concert, adopting the adage that the way you do one thing is the way you do everything.

♓ PISCES

Capricorn's hard lines and limits can sometimes feel like anathema to mermaid Pisces. But January actually invites you to get courageous with your containers, by saying no when needed and by checking in to, rather than out from, whatever challenges are presenting in your life.

✦ With roll-the-dice Jupiter gearing up for its victory lap through your sign, January finds you comfy in the driver's seat, as you allow yourself to shine and take the wheel with both hands.

♈ ARIES

Cardinal babes are born to move and groove it, and both Aries and Capricorn like to prove their survivalist chops by taking life by the horns. January's energy asks you to savour some slowness in this process, as you adopt and adapt to Capricorn's brick-by-brick trajectory and trust the results of your actions to unfold in their own sweet time.

✦ With your ruling planet, Mars, heading through fellow Fire sign Sagittarius until the 24th, January wants to remind you that you're here to be our poster child of power. This means using your force with generosity, and battling it out in the service of what's best for all.

♉ TAURUS

Both touchably luxe advocates of this tasty world, Taurus energy is the rustic farmhouse dinner to Capricorn's Michelin-starred meal. Use January to raise the bar a notch, elevating your goals from the same old salad bar of options and imagining the *amuse-bouche* of your high-end dreams.

✦ As Uranus stations direct in your sign, you're invited to loosen your grip in all arenas. Begin by looking back into your life archive and tracking your life/death/rebirth cycles. Wherever you are in this cocoon-to-butterfly process right now, throw a party for your current incarnation.

♊ GEMINI

Your vibes are all high tops and backpacks, while stately Capricorn feels better in a grown-up gown. Take this season to sample a flavour of maturity that feels potent rather than patriarchal by slipping into a silky button-up blouse that soothes some of your nervous energy without stifling it.

✦ With your ruler, Mercury, rolling retrograde through Aquarius this month, it's high time to get prophetic, exploring plans and projects that transcend your usual buzzy immediacy in favour of a longer-term vision.

♋ CANCER

Sitting opposite one another on the zodiac wheel, Capricorn and Cancer energies both awaken themes of shelter and belonging. January invites you to structure your flow, considering when to step out from the hidden emotional swirl to own the force of your feelings, harnessing them to navigate decision-making in the world at large.

✦ This month's Full Moon in your sign asks you to share the sensations in your secret diary, considering how you might expand the inner circle of your trusted few to invite more hearts to witness the wonder of you.

♌ LEO

Capricorn energy can sometimes feel like it's calling time on your endless days in the sun. But the treasures of January ask you to sweep your regal, hot-pink mane into an updo that's equal parts irresistible and utilitarian, sampling the strength that can stem from a little self-restraint.

✦ This month's energy asks us to high-step beyond the ego, which can be a challenge for Leo's special sparkles. Imagine you're the ghostwriter of your own life. Where can you trust so deeply in your impact that you don't even have to sign your name?

♍ VIRGO

Both Earth signs, Virgo and Capricorn know the pleasure of self-powered precision. January invites you to build on this foundation, as you break ranks with the endless cycle of refinement and simply come out with it already, laying a risky claim to a project or partnership that's yours and yours alone.

✦ Your ruler Mercury's roll through the eccentric electricity of Aquarius beckons you to deepen your relationship to badass solitude, trusting individualistic inner visions even if you can't yet explain them to the world.

♎ LIBRA

The more reserved of the Cardinal signs, both Libra and Capricorn dance a fine line between 'should' and 'want'. January invites you to seize greater control of this divide, calling the shots and pledging allegiance to your needs, even when you risk challenging your established image.

✦ As your ruler, Venus, travels retro for most of the month in Capricorn, this is a potent moment for rediscovering your inner pleasure centre. What longings have you been keeping under wraps that are ready to be owned?

♏ SCORPIO

Accustomed to rugged, raw reality, both Scorpio and Capricorn can make like cacti and weather any dry times. Let January be your crown jewels as you harness your penchant for power moves in a more public-facing way, making sweet love to your own ambitions without apology.

✦ As the Sun meets up with your ruler, deliciously down-and-dirty Pluto, at mid-month, ask yourself where you're ready for part of you to 'die', composting a habit or behavioural pattern in service of new blooms.

↗ SAGITTARIUS

When Sagittarius' wild ponies face Capricorn's corralling energy, this Fire sign's unbridled sense of expansion is asked to take it slow and steady. Let January feel like an elaborate exercise in suitcase-packing, as you discover delight in the process of preparing for your next adventure.

✦ With move-it Mars racing through your sign for most of the month, it's a fine time to calibrate the rhythm of your actions and reactions, deciding exactly how much speed and pressure to apply to each aspect of your life.

STAR STYLE

COLOUR: Cover yourself in Old Hollywood hues fit for a self-sufficient starlet in the decadent dead of winter. Think carmine red, jade green, aubergine, ivory, champagne, sumptuous black velvet and shimmery steel.

FASHION: Model yourself after a mash-up of Marlene Dietrich in *Shanghai Express*, Sharon Stone in *Basic Instinct*, and après-ski wear, complete with smoking jackets, high-waisted trousers, silk dressing gowns, floor-length faux-fur coats, designer handbags and your sharpest stilettos. Whatever sartorial style you select, find support in the structure of impeccable tailoring, custom cuts and signature silhouettes.

SCENT: January's aromas are hard-earned, hedonistically *haute* and lavishly timeless. Think Chanel No. 5, frankincense oil, pine, cigar smoke and 'grown-up' scents remembered from childhood.

FOOD FOR THE SOUL

Build your empire of fortified body sustainability with mature, expensive flavours fit for an alpine castle, such as bone broth, cave-aged cheese, caviar, rare vintages, root-vegetable juice, hot cocoa and truffles.

CHART YOUR COURSE

January's energies connect us to peaks, pinnacles and palatial places.
Consider a medieval Croatian city with rocky outcrops, a foray into
the mountainous majesty of St Moritz or an opera performed in
a Venetian palazzo on the Grand Canal. And if a long flight isn't
on the cards, explore gates, walls, fortifications and historic homes
near where you live, discovering your town's outer limits, seats of
power and most consistently coveted hot spots.

ELEMENTAL EXCURSIONS

Cardinal Earth-sign-ruled January is made for luxurious treatments
as well as rugged empire building. Think entrepreneurial courses,
wilderness survival schools, fencing lessons, body-rocking boot
camps, ski lodge getaways, ice baths, elaborate manicures and
acupuncture, creating your own capsule collection and high-end
spa days.

PLANETARY PROMPTS

Use these magic words and journal
questions to moor you this month...

SELF-SOVEREIGNTY:

Where can I call the shots and 'back' myself?

OWNERSHIP:

What area of my life is ready to be
competently 'claimed'?

STANDARDS:

What is my personal definition of success and
how can I celebrate both inner and outer 'wins'?

GRIT:

In the event of the apocalypse, which of my
inner qualities would help me survive?

LEGACY:

What do I want to leave behind and how can
I consciously contribute to this in the present-day?

MONDAY	TUESDAY	WEDNESDAY	THURSDAY	FRIDAY	SATURDAY	SUNDAY
	1 FEBRUARY New Moon in Aquarius			**4 FEBRUARY** Mercury stations direct in Capricorn		**6 FEBRUARY** Mars in Capricorn square Chiron in Aries
					12 FEBRUARY Pluto in Capricorn trine the North Node in Taurus	
		16 FEBRUARY Full Moon in Leo		**18 FEBRUARY** Sun enters Pisces		

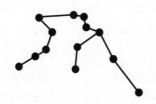

FEBRUARY

CHARGE YOUR
SPIRITUAL CIRCUITRY

CHARGE YOUR
SPIRITUAL CIRCUITRY

Clear out and clean out to catalyse a change. February's astrology is a sweep and a swoop and a snap-crackle-pop of cosmic medicine that shoots straight through our hearts, into our veins and out into the world without hesitation.

It's a month for acts of reformation and re-creation, as we recharge our battery packs and ready ourselves for our next incarnation. Injected with the unstoppable innovations of Aquarius, the penultimate sign of the zodiac, February skyrockets us towards our most out-there imaginings. It's a move-it-and-shake-it moment to practise getting out of our own way.

In the wheel of the year, Aquarius is our final Fixed sign (following Taurus, Leo and Scorpio). This energy beckons us to accept ourselves fully, taking a leap into the unfettered aliveness and eccentricity of exactly who and what we are.

As we reach the close of the astrological year, which ends next month in Pisces, we are asked to become lighter and looser, tossing any heavy baggage by the wayside. Figuring out how to land the electrical Aquarian energy, which is often described in outer-space terms of alien detachment, can be hard back down here on Earth.

But this sign and this month are here to help us consider our place within the whole and to move us beyond where we could go alone.

Think back to a time when you couldn't possibly have envisioned that you'd be where you are right now. Consider the confluence of things – all the pieces and parts – that had to conspire to bring you to this crossroads. How many of these influences were so far outside of your control that you could never have seen them coming? And now look around at your world today, at all that's coming together and falling apart to come back together again, and notice the way that plans and partnerships take and change shape. February wants you to connect with this bird's eye view of your bold new world.

In the Tarot, this month is guided by The Star card, a no-nonsense healer that descends into our dens with charged-up cleaning tools, ready to reconnect us to the source. What is ripe for a reset in your world? What particles that might be impeding mobility are trapped in your life-filter right now? February urges you to power-vacuum every corner of your world without getting hung up on what may be lost in the process. It's a month to banish sentimentality and aim your precious life-force beams towards the new.

A neon light on the horizon, February wants you to journey to the edge of what you know and take a leap, coming unstuck and charting an as-yet unmapped course. Your existence is more deliciously strange than you could possibly imagine. And it's time to Electric Slide into the embrace of the future you.

FEBRUARY DATES WITH DESTINY: COMMIT TO THE CLEARING

With all the planets in forward motion, all stellar systems are cleared for take-off. Paired with some steady-on Earth energies, there's no messing around this February, which sees us ready to wake up and commit to consciously shaking away any sense of stuckness. But rather than a tough-love football coach who forces our muscles past our bodily limits, February 2022 helps us to make some clean and easy breaks.

Take this month to call it quits on something without beating yourself up with tired tales of wasted time and self-incriminating regret. What if you could just **slip out the back door on an old habit or pattern that's no longer of service**, disappearing into the night like a sleepwalker in search of a new dream?

Let February help you pivot towards the new, as you focus on all that's coming into relief through your cosmic camera lens.

New Moon in Aquarius

CLEAN AND FRESH: This Aquarius lunar event is an invigorating ice bath of renewal. The New Moon asks you to **consider the concepts of space and spaciousness, taking time away, apart and above it all.** Get strategic and play with the geometrics of your life, looking at how each part and person affect the whole. This Moon wants us to mastermind our lives without getting manipulative. Make aspirational adjustments with clear eyes and a commitment to your inner oracle, trusting that you already 'know' the right moves to make.

Mercury stations direct in Capricorn
(re-enters Aquarius on 14th)

NOISE-CANCELLING HEADPHONES: Mercury's retrograde roll between Capricorn and Aquarius has asked us to consciously choose what we're picking up from our energetic and mental environments. With this metabolic planet now stationing direct (think of this as a gear shift), now is a moment for choosing a form of noise-cancelling headphones. **What stories and situations are you simply not available to take in any more?** Drop any drama around the fallout from saying a sovereign 'no', and revel in how some black-and-white borders can make your personal rainbow feel more vivid.

Mars in Capricorn square Chiron in Aries

NO MORE PROVING: Along with Saturn, Jupiter and the North Node, the planetoid Chiron is part of our 'soul school'. But while the other planets have us hitting the gym as we strive towards self-sufficiency, with Chiron we're asked to engage in a different form of work. This touchy-feely soft spot urges us to abide with the full range of our humanness as if nothing needs to be 'fixed'. Today's face-off between go-getter Mars in mountaineering Capricorn and empathy-seeking Chiron in me-focused Aries asks us to **confront any lack of compassion we have for ourselves head-on**, diving into the feelings that lie beneath our need to constantly prove it.

Pluto in Capricorn trine the North Node in Taurus

YOU ARE THE SOURCE: They might use different means of medicine, but underworld Pluto and pie-in-the-sky North Node share a desire to lift us towards our highest potential. This meeting in the earthy energies of Capricorn and Taurus is here to help us investigate our base survival fears and our soul's yearnings. Start by looking at any person, institution or project that you perceive to be your 'source' of something, and discover how **relying on an external entity to confirm your worthiness strips you of your belief in your own**

inherent bounty. Remind yourself that nothing and no one has the power to give or take away your inner shelter and security.

Full Moon in Leo

LOVE WITHOUT LIMITS: Each Full Moon is a face-off between two astrological signs that exist together on a polarity. Aquarius and its opposite, Leo, speak to the heart and veins: Leo is the heart, powering us with feline flair, while Aquarius circulates the life-giving essence of our creativity to the world. Take this Moon to consider **how and what you can love louder and without limits.** Aim to strike a balance between heart-on-the-sleeve ardour and the trust that this love can live without your having to stake your claim.

Sun enters Pisces

LOSE SIGHT OF DRY LAND: As we transition from Aquarius into Pisces, we're invited to soften our strategic minds as we **find delight in the feeling of getting just a little bit 'lost'.** Start by noticing where you've become attached to a particular vision or outcome. Where is your urge to make rational 'sense' of things keeping you from your emotional sense? Open wide to more aquatic ways of knowing, letting whatever's not meant to stay simply slip out of view.

STAR PARTY:
IMBOLC (1 FEBRUARY)

One of the cross-quarter holidays in the Pagan 'Wheel of the Year', this festival was originally associated with the goddess Brigid. A poetic priestess who watched over all 'high country' – from hills to uplands to wishes for what 'could be' – Brigid's all-seeing energy syncs with the prescient power of genius Greek goddess Athena. The storied lore of Imbolc shows February as a time for taking an elevated approach to our lives, as we engage in cleanings and clearings and seek a heightened consciousness to lift us up to where we can envision what comes next.

SIGN-BY-SIGN
GUIDE TO FEBRUARY

♒ AQUARIUS

It's your season, vital visionary! Aquarian birds of all feathers are bound by the shared impulse to create space, and February asks you to step into this mission with a sense of stillness. Begin by noticing any 'noise' that might be creating static in your nervous system. Honour your urges to just get away from it all – saying 'no' to any external commitments that feel like they're taking up all available space in your life in favour of seeking internal spaciousness. Don't be afraid to take time away from anything taxing, including tech. Amplify your inner voice instead this month, letting the sweet silence open your mental skies to new schemes that spring straight from your third eye.

✦ As planets in your sign mix with Earth energies this month, February asks you to consider your 'source' – exploring the iron-rich attributes of your core self that have transcended time and space, and letting these qualities lead you back to what restores and replenishes your energy. Whether it's a petal-powered bubble bath, a quarter-pounder with fries, or streaking naked through the woods, trust that your self-caretaking can be as weirdly and wonderfully individual as you.

♓ PISCES

Both Pisces and Aquarius are 'out-there' explorers who exist to break boundaries and uncover oneness with the world. Take February to remember your role as medium – a relayer of messages – and treat this month like a personal séance, allowing cosmic energy to flow through you freely without getting stuck in earthly dramas.

✦ With a sweet meet-up this month between your ruler, dream queen Neptune, and the pillow princess of receiving, Venus, February is your moment to practise swapping out some of your sacrificial energy to let others bend the knee.

♈ ARIES

Aries and Aquarius are both renegade-flavoured first-responders who arrive on the scene to awaken and invigorate. February's energies ask you to consider the rippling impact of your force, balancing your sometimes reckless, see-if-it-sticks spaghetti moves with some more strategic savvy.

✦ With a tender meet-up between Chiron in your sign and your ruler, Mars, February asks you to explore when your urge to be hard as nails might hide some softer yearnings underneath, balancing your steel with some silky sensitivity.

♉ TAURUS

Fixed sign energies here to build power from the inside out, both Taurus and Aquarius connect us to the seat of our very vitality. February's energies invite you to consider your root system more closely, as you commit to clearing out any faulty foundations and building anew upon solid stone.

✦ This month's meet-up between Pluto in Capricorn and the North Node in your sign wants to connect you with a more evolutionary sense of worthiness, as you're asked to interrogate who and what you let define your sense of 'good enough'.

♊ GEMINI

Both Air babes here in service of gathering intel, Gemini and Aquarius are poised to draw dazzling connections between people, places and ideas. Let the Fixed Aquarius form of Air soothe your nervous system this month and allow the chorus of voices around and inside you to settle before you try to translate.

✦ With your ruler, Mercury, now rolling forwards once again, consider how you metabolize your messaging this month. Take time to assimilate and sift through your experiences and gather your mission statements with the power of a podium speaker.

♋ CANCER

Infused with a dose of limitless lunacy, Cancer and Aquarius are both endowed with the gift of pure imagination. Let your capacity for fantasy unstick you from the past this month, as you mix the sepia-toned photographs of your memory with the knowledge that no matter what the flashbacks, you are always moving forwards.

✦ Ruled by the Moon, the monthly lunar cycle is forever yours for the treasuring. In February, this cycle asks you to remember your rightful role as creator of your own reality – slipping into the seams of your self-sewn smock with empowered artistry.

♌ LEO

A beautiful balancing act between the personal and the communal, Leo and Aquarius are both key players in the creative process. Take February to explore how you can make your presence felt without pushing, trusting that your warmth keeps the room lit when you simply show up.

✦ The Full Moon in your sign this month asks you to open up to a lighter way of loving. Consider how to soften some of your jungle prowess and be more like a house cat – letting your lust draw the milk into your lap rather than stalking your prey.

♍ VIRGO

Lean and keen seers who can read the environmental cues in an instant, both Virgo and Aquarius have a clear grasp of their part within the whole. February asks you to experiment with your 'range' – tapping into your vast array of possibilities before you commit to any prescriptive paths.

✦ This month adds a richer Earth flavour to the usual Airy February feel, and you're asked to become grounded accordingly, acting from a place of physical instinct as you choose where to devote your precious resources.

♎ LIBRA

Both Libra and Aquarius are truth speakers and idealized realists, looking at what's here squarely in the eye in order to bring about change. February invites you to break free of any endless back-and-forth efforts to keep the peace during this process of truth seeking, rocking the boat to find a more ecstatic form of equilibrium.

✦ With your ruler, Venus, getting cosy with dream-keeper Neptune this month, consider how to invite a more expansive sense of allowing into your relationships, moving beyond any rigid expectations as you choose to let others surprise you.

♏ SCORPIO

While Scorpio tends towards the more carnivorous and Aquarius the more cerebral, both trailblaze where others might be too timid to tread. February invites you to consider how to 'cool' some of your carnal desires – simply pursuing your passions and making any necessary course corrections, without having to wage a life-and-death struggle.

◆ With the North Node in your opposite sign of Taurus now activated, it's a month for coming up to the surface. Save your deep-diving scuba suit for another season and choose to enjoy the present with the fullness of your presence.

♐ SAGITTARIUS

Sagittarius and Aquarius share an endless urge for expansion – perpetually poised to race down the next open road. February asks you to consider how to codify all that endless experiential energy, drawing upon your Technicolor fountain of hard-earned life wisdom without having to look beyond your own power pool for the answers.

◆ As your ruler, Jupiter, sextiles Uranus mid-month, February is made for embracing your own brand of intuitive genius. Pay attention to how 'hits' of inspiration and intel come to you, letting mysterious knowledge motivate your next move.

♑ CAPRICORN

Both originally ruled by cosmic CEO Saturn, Capricorn and Aquarius share a penchant for interrogating structure and form. Take February to explore the notion of tradition and inheritance, tracing the pathways that motivate your behavioural responses and assessing which parts of your metaphorical house are ready for a renovation.

✦ As Pluto in your sign meets the North Node, take this time to consider when an insatiable appetite for 'more' sometimes leaves you feeling 'less'. Shifting out of acquisitions mode can give you space to consider the resources already on your table.

STAR STYLE

COLOUR: Step into a chic chemistry lab of newborn neons and clear futures with white vinyl, platinum, lightning-bolt lemon, aluminium sparkle, see-through shades and green-lit chartreuse.

FASHION: Revolutionize your look with Ziggy Stardust meets Willy Wonka at Burning Man attire. Think dandy leisurewear, moon booties, mile-high platforms, visionary glasses, puffer jackets and political pins and patches. Whatever you sport, consider fabrics that are eco-conscious and aerodynamic – empowering you to leave a light footprint as you rocket through the world.

SCENT: February's aromas are metallic and invigoratingly innovative – think wintergreen, aldehyde-based perfumes, aromatic aquatic fragrances, the air after a lightning storm or the spacious smell of an empty room.

FOOD FOR THE SOUL

Supercharge your system with piquant 'wake-up call' treats, breakthrough culinary adventures and planet-friendly bites. Think pure matcha, wasabi peas, star fruit, soapy coriander, lime, astronaut ice cream, cricket flour and hydroponic sprouts.

CHART YOUR COURSE

February's energies connect us to spacious skies and the renegade
room to move. Explore the endlessness of the Great Plains, the
edge-of-the-world energies of Big Sur or the advanced modernity
of Singapore. For an Aquarian voyage a bit closer to home, consider
any big expanse in your area – be it a recreation ground, baseball
diamond, cricket pitch, performance arena or citywide bus system
– that awakens a sense of al fresco dynamics and interconnectivity.

ELEMENTAL EXCURSIONS

Fixed Air-sign-ruled February is made for cool consideration and
alternative communions. Think aviation, cloud-watching, vista
points, planetariums, space-clearing, house renovations, juice
cleanses, plant medicine, sober raves, experimental art, electronic
beats, future labs and scientific exploration.

PLANETARY PROMPTS

Use these magic words and journal
questions to moor you this month…

REORIENTATION:

Where do I get 'stuck' in life and how can I
practise getting out of my own way?

REINVENTION:

What is my relationship to change and
how might I evolve this approach?

CLEARING:

How can I reset, recharge and 'return' to myself?

VISION:

Where can I take things less personally and
adopt a more panned-out perspective?

SPACE:

How do I 'take up' space? How much space do I
need? And how do I access this spaciousness?

MONDAY	TUESDAY	WEDNESDAY	THURSDAY	FRIDAY	SATURDAY	SUNDAY
		2 MARCH New Moon in Pisces				**6 MARCH** Venus + Mars enter Aquarius
			10 MARCH Mercury enters Pisces			**13 MARCH** Sun conjunct Neptune in Pisces
				18 MARCH Full Moon in Virgo		**20 MARCH** Sun enters Aries
28 MARCH Venus conjunct Saturn in Aquarius						

MARCH

EVERY LOSS
IS A FIND

EVERY LOSS
IS A FIND

A weepy ending and an eternal return, the astrology of March is both fathomless and synthesizing – our chance to soften all our edges and fade into the ether of absolute allowing.

Ushered in by the energy of Pisces, the 12th and final sign of the zodiac, this is the end of the astrological year. Holding it all and then some, this holy heart-melter of a month is vaster than the ocean of emotion itself, beckoning us into a more expansive way of being that leaves nothing out. Everything is everything, and it's all a part of you, says Pisces. March invites us to sync to the vibration of every pulse – with no defences between ourselves and all that surrounds us.

In the Tarot, Pisces is watched over by The Moon card. A mysterious lunar landscape of bumps in the night, The Moon's insistent whisper urges us to follow the intuitive pull of our inner longing. Take this time to both lose your way and find it again, as you learn to float instead of force, navigating by tender surrendered feeling alone.

We hear a lot about 'letting go' and getting 'over it', setting our stopwatches as we await the day that we'll finally be 'done' with

M

whatever we perceive as needing to be fixed or purged from our lives. But the energy of March asks us to do ourselves one better than seeking neat and tidy 'closure'. Inviting us to simply be with our process as it all unfolds, March says to get under it, get beside it, move with it.

What are you longing to be finished with right now? And what keeps coming back of its own accord, like some kind of boomerang? Could you look it in the eyes without shame? Could you reach out to touch it and ask it what it wants to share, committing to walk alongside it for as long as it likes? This month asks us to make peace with the parts of our lives and ourselves that we fear will never ever be 'complete'.

March and Pisces remind us that we control next to nothing in this life, and that claiming our exhilarating insignificance within the whole is how we actually uncover our own omnipotence. When we commit to staying with every last sensation of our precious aliveness, we become holy in our humanness.

The invitation this month is to let this world do its work upon you. To slip and slide into unseen realms with salt-kissed skin that's made from the stars themselves. It is a time to let what is already leaving you learn how to swim.

MARCH DATES WITH DESTINY:
FEEL IT TO HEAL IT

As the sensitive surrealism of Pisces collides with the clear-eyed cleansing of Aquarius and the organic order of Virgo, March 2022 produces a powerful poultice for any open wounds. It's a moment for facing what we might not have wanted to see about our lives and **inviting any perceived 'brokenness' in from the storm for reparation and healing.**

Start by gently looking through your peephole at any feelings you have left outside in the cold. Do you perceive this part of you as a pathology in yourself that must be exorcised from your daily existence? Do you find yourself searching for the cause of the pain while actually evading the teachings of the sensation itself?

Pay attention to your patterns, let yourself be 'in process' and mix up some merciful magic as you prepare your own proprietary bundle of healing herbs with equal parts of courage and compassion.

New Moon in Pisces

THE SOFT LAUNCH: Emerging from the ethereal haze of the Waning Moon period, the Pisces New Moon is embryonic – a chance to explore how **we can initiate from a much less pushy place than we might be used to.** Take this time to tune in to how you apply your energy at the very beginning of a project or partnership, noticing when you might rush to define the contours before you let what's naturally coming into form show itself to you. And as you 'begin', remember what is ending as you birth the new, staying close to the spiral of your life and being careful not to force yourself to forge ahead without taking all your past lives along for the ride.

Venus + Mars enter Aquarius

THE PASSION ORACLE: Both Venus and Mars connect us to our desire centre. Venus does so through dilation and receiving, opening us up to be able to take in and absorb pleasure. And Mars does it through activation and ignition, firing up the engine of our inner huntress to seek and obtain what we crave. As these two planets shift into all-seeing Aquarius, any cravings cool down and we are asked to consider the far-reaching impact of our hungers. But rather than stifle your longings, take this time to treat your wants and needs like a deck of oracle cards. **Notice what and whom you reach for, and check in with what this reveals** about where you are in your life right now and where you're heading. From the literal spices and sweets you pop into your mouth, to the golden goals that rev your engine, each desire wants to tell you a secret about yourself.

Mercury enters Pisces
(enters Aries on 27th)

WHISPERS OF THE WORLD: As mental and metabolic Mercury slides into the sign of mysterious whispers, this planetary passage is an opportunity to consider how we can tune in more deeply to the tides of our lives. Notice when you gather information like a vacuum cleaner – simply sucking info in to immediately make a 'rational' decision – and when you might race to declare something before allowing yourself a pause to process and integrate an experience. Take this transit to **let life 'talk back' to you, allowing for plenty of soft silence so that the signs and symbols feel safe to reveal themselves**. When Mercury heats up in Fire sign Aries on the 27th, you'll be ready to sing your message loud and proud once again.

Sun conjunct Neptune in Pisces

ROLE PLAY: Gauzy Neptune, ruler of Pisces, is our planetary sweet escape – a one-way ticket past the end of the rainbow that asks us to come undone and get carried away without needing to understand 'why'. And as this planet touches up on the Sun – representing the fierce individuation point of our singular self – we have a chance to shade the pastels of our personhood. **Where have you become attached to the hard lines and limits of your identity?** What roles are you ready to release? Let this transit be your permission slip to slide into a more relaxed stance, as you no longer feel the need to 'hold it together' and keep up a brave face to make others comfortable.

Full Moon in Virgo

TAKE THE SHAPE: Seated at the opposite end of the spectrum from Pisces, Virgo is the discerning sieve to the blended Pisces soup. Sorting, refining and deciding what snacks will bring true sustenance, the sign of the witch and the herbalist forges our fierce inner code and watches over our portals – deciding what matters most. This Moon is an intricate opportunity to consider the concept of devotion in your life, **carefully selecting what to submit**

to without losing one drop of your power. Where could you 'take the shape' around something that's occurring right now, allowing it to do its work on you while retaining your personal agency?

Sun enters Aries

SOMETHING OUT OF NOTHING: One of the most bracing, emboldened transitions of the astrological year, the shift from Pisces into original life-force Aries is nothing short of miraculous. Consider this moment your 'big bang' and feel for the gap between seeming nothingness and everything exploding into being. Look around you, whichever hemisphere you live in, and notice what has been sleeping just beneath the surface – what is taking a deep in-breath before it bursts into song? As we're poised to shoot out of the starting gate into Aries country, give yourself a few final moments to **honour the gorgeous gap that exists between endings and beginnings.**

Venus conjunct Saturn in Aquarius

EXPAND YOUR PALATE: Before astronomers discovered change-maker Uranus, Aquarius was ruled by the rooted regalness of Saturn, and today the sign pays homage to both planets – divining when to travel past the edge of the known and when to rein it in and hold its form. As Aquarius hosts pleasure-principle Venus along with its old mentor, we're asked to examine **the balance between the creature comforts we automatically reach for and the palate-expanders that will take us towards greater evolutionary growth.** Notice where an old source of sustenance has lost its flavour and commit to slowly introducing some new spices into your life.

M

STAR PARTY:
EQUINOX (20 MARCH)

Rooted in the Latin term for 'equal day and night', the equinox marks the moment when the Sun crosses the celestial equator and day and night are equal in length. The spring equinox in the northern hemisphere, or the autumn equinox in the southern hemisphere, occurs on 20 March with the Sun's ingress into Aries. (The other equinox falls on 23 September.) This is a potent portal for examining our own dualities, as we're guided by Aries and the Tarot's Emperor card. It is a time to take up the space you merit, and also to examine the responsibility that comes with being you. This first equinox of the year is meant for exploring how you make your mark.

SIGN-BY-SIGN
GUIDE TO MARCH

♓ PISCES

Happy birthday season, sweet seaweed babe! Your sign often seeks to elude life's grip, slipping and sliding away into the escape of elsewhere. This month, take a look at where you 'go' in these moments of metaphorical dream vacation, making your energy needs clear to yourself and others and exploring the fine line between avoidance and self-advocacy. Ask yourself whether you're ghosting something because you fear a direct confrontation, and whether a departure feels more like an energetic elopement that lets you reforge your commitment to self-love. You have every right to stage an off-grid getaway or go radio-silent as needed, so long as your urge to check out is something you are consciously choosing.

✦ As the Sun in your sign makes some supportive aspects to Uranus, the North Node and Pluto, consider your relationship to your own expansion this month. Where are you growing out of your usual soul clothing right now? Wherever you find yourself in your growth cycle, stay soft around your notion of progress, checking any urge to chastise yourself for leaning back on old habits or patterns as you transition. Remind yourself that, just like the motion of breathing, the rhythm of expansion is both in and out, and there is no such thing as falling behind.

♈ ARIES

Sitting side by side, Aries and Pisces are buddies who govern the final curtain call of the astrological year and the fresh new beginning, respectively. Let March be your chance to wait in the wings with both anticipation and a calm sense of inner timing, poised to enter at exactly the right moment.

✦ As your ruler, Mars, meets up with Venus in Aquarius, it's a month made for widening your field of wants. Balance any desirous tunnel visions with some off-road pleasures, even if they don't immediately seem to serve your end goal.

♉ TAURUS

The lickable spoon and the meltable ice cream, Taurus and Pisces both love to absorb life's sweet sensations. March is your moment to move beyond the material and into the subtler pleasures of the invisible realm, remembering that there's just as much joy to be found in what cannot be named as there is in the stuff we cling on to.

✦ As your ruler, Venus, travels through spacious Aquarius, it's a time for unclutching your pleasure purse and giving your passions more room to roam. Allow yourself to discover that loosening some of the laws around love can let in more ardour.

♊ GEMINI

Like breathable fabrics that curiously absorb each environmental aroma, both Gemini and Pisces are born to sample every shade of the rainbow. Let March remind you that you have the right to drop out to power up in this process of sampling – leaving the party when you've had enough without fear of missing out.

+ As this month's Moon cycle awakens you to subtle body signals, consider the dynamics of your personal biosphere. Pay close attention to how certain people, places and patterns actually make you feel and making any adjustments accordingly.

♋ CANCER

Two salt-soaked sirens who are comfy in the emo deep end, Cancer and Pisces are here to be saturated in the waters that swirl within. Embrace the magic mutability of Pisces, letting sensations move through you like mist, without getting stuck in any tangly tidal pools.

+ The Moon cycle this month gets extra juice from intuitive meaning-maker Jupiter. You're invited into an optimistic expansion of your understanding of the realms of possibility. Whatever is on the brink of being birthed in your world deserves a celebratory welcome party.

♌ LEO

The invisible ink to Leo's permanent marker, Pisces is here to help Leo explore the space between acts of self-expression and the inevitable evanescence of our specialness. Take March to practise resting in the afterglow of what you've already made before you chase the next creative high.

✦ As your ruler, the Sun, meets up with both Jupiter and Neptune this month, it's prime time to expand and reinvent your concept of self. Swap rigid adherence to affirmations of 'I am' with the more mutable magic of 'all that I might be'.

♍ VIRGO

Partners in manifestation who bow to every precious particle of the Universe, both Virgo and Pisces are here to sense and respond to each shift in the cosmic weather. Let March be your invitation into a more immersive experience – forgoing your usual methodology for a magical ride through the beautiful chaos.

✦ As your ruler, Mercury, meets up with both Uranus and the North Node in fellow Earth signs, you're asked to initiate a change at your own pace. Even if it's taking one baby step down the spiral staircase, trust that every micro-movement matters.

♎ LIBRA

Idealistic dreamers who can find the silver linings in the cloudiest of skies, both Libra and Pisces are here to lift and elevate us all above the humdrum. In March, add some Piscean fantasia to your more pragmatic visions, letting your castle come into view without having to manage its construction site.

◆ With a series of meet-ups this month between your ruler, Venus, and the 'outer' planets of evolutionary change, think about how you can let yourself get a little bit carried away – opening up to whatever wants to move you.

♏ SCORPIO

Scorpio and Pisces both swim with the fishes in the deep blue sea, endlessly called to plunge into profundity and to *feel* more and more. Use this month to learn a thing or two from a mistier, more Piscean form of emotional fusion, forgoing some of your usual fears about others' hidden motivations and allowing your trusting heart to open like a flower, no matter what the risk.

◆ As the Sun meets up with your honorary ruler, the lunar point Lilith (the point at which the Moon is furthest from the Earth), March is a month made for finding the fierceness in forgiveness.

Acceptance doesn't have to equal powerlessness. Instead, let it give you the courage to hold the whole storm within you.

♐ SAGITTARIUS

Wildly kinetic cosmic kids who move through the world with wonder and awe, both Pisces and Sagittarius are here to widen your gaze and trip away – picking whichever path beckons. Let March reconnect you to your love of surprise endings, as you question any places where you think you know it all and stay open to astonishment.

✦ As Mercury in Pisces starts a dynamic conversation with your sign this month, explore the speed at which you assimilate your experiences, noticing when you might need a little more time to integrate before springing into immediate action.

♑ CAPRICORN

The motivated morning run to the little mermaid's slumber, clear-cut Capricorn and this maker of magic can help each other find the balance between structure and dissolution. Let March invite you to follow the line of least resistance for a change, releasing the belief that your worth must always be built out of long and protracted labour.

+ As your ruler, Saturn, heads towards a meeting with Venus, it's a month made for committing for the long haul. Examine anything you're currently carrying that you wouldn't want by your side in the apocalypse, and then carefully, tenderly, set it down and carry on.

♒ AQUARIUS

Sharing a penchant for pushing the boundaries, both Aquarius and Pisces work actively with all that is unknown. Let this month be an exercise in shifting from your usual 'seeing' to a more amorphous 'sensing', as you let yourself be guided beyond the limits without having to rationalize your liberation.

+ With Venus and Mars meeting up in your sign, you are invited to explore the balance between having and getting. Notice when it's time to consciously initiate a mission and when you can allow your acquisitions to be brought your way by life instead.

STAR STYLE

COLOUR: Let your shades be softly lit, aquatically artful and translucently transcendent, with barely-there blush and interiors decorated in shades of opalescent cream, pearl bisque, misty moss, sea-foam green, lilac and turquoise ombré and iridescent mussel.

FASHION: Channel an aesthetic meet-up between Ibiza chic and the little mermaid in Malibu with bandeau bras, body glitter, diaphanous drapery, dewy skin, nude bodysuits, balayage highlights, beachcomber jeans and waterproof plastic jelly shoes. Whatever you wear, let it be loose and layered – reminding yourself that you can always slip in and out of any skin.

SCENT: March's aromas are mistily mystical and subtly spirit-lifting – think wet, mossy chypre perfumes and heady incense – or simply inhale whatever exists in the air at this moment, tapping into the ever-shifting olfactory climate of your current environment.

FOOD FOR THE SOUL

The bites of Pisces season are amorphous, fusible and tastily transportive: think kombucha, gem-infused lattes, seaweed, foam and froth, and fantasy foods like candyfloss and angel food cake.

CHART YOUR COURSE

The energy of March indoctrinates us into dazzling macrocosmic moments when we can abandon the map. Explore dream getaways and cruises, and visit fairy-tale book and film locations. Closer to home, you can dip into any liminal zones – playing in places where the clear boundaries between neighbourhoods blur or solid land gives way to the sea. Immerse yourself in spatial 'overwhelm' by wandering crowded streets or hiking at the foot of mountains, where you can find delight in becoming deliriously dot-sized.

ELEMENTAL EXCURSIONS

Mutable Water sign-ruled March is made for blending our borders and releasing the to-do lists as we come utterly undone. Think sensory-deprivation tanks, sound baths, stargazing, transcendental meditation, silent retreats, fantasy suites, elopements, cuddle parties and unscheduled blank spaces.

PLANETARY PROMPTS

Use these magic words and journal
questions to moor you this month…

ALLOWING:

Which parts of me are ready to be felt rather than fixed?

MELTING:

Where can I stop trying so hard and soften instead?

MERGING:

How can I listen more deeply to my own life's
wisdom, and how does the world 'talk' to me?

ENDINGS:

How can I honour what's passing away
without forcing myself to 'get over it'?

RELEASE:

What does my personal style of 'letting go' look like?

MONDAY	TUESDAY	WEDNESDAY	THURSDAY	FRIDAY	SATURDAY	SUNDAY
				1 APRIL New Moon in Aries		
	5 APRIL Venus enters Pisces					
11 APRIL Mercury enters Taurus				**15 APRIL** Mars enters Pisces	**16 APRIL** Full Moon in Libra	
		20 APRIL Sun enters Taurus				
				29 APRIL Pluto stations retrograde in Capricorn	**30 APRIL** New Moon in Taurus (partial solar eclipse)	

APRIL

COME ALIVE AGAIN

COME ALIVE
AGAIN

A cayenne pepper-spiced clarion call at dawn break, April's astrology is red-hot and ready – bursting through the pavement cracks like irresistibly emboldened sprouting plants.

Bringing us back to the beginning of the astrological wheel of the year, April's energy is governed by the very first sign of them all: Aries. The originating matchstick that ignites the whole shebang, Aries marks our innocent, exuberant initiation down the birth canal – a process that is at once inevitable, exhilarating and exhausting, as we unabashedly declare our arrival on the scene.

Ruled by engine-revving Mars, April's energy can sometimes feel penetrative, awakening our urge to puncture the planet with unchecked force, determined to make our mark, no matter what. But at its core, April asks us to get lean and stripped-down, coming ever closer to our aerodynamic essence, quick and firefly-fit – think of this month as your sinewy spark plug. With nothing to lose and everything to give, April is made for aligning with the barefaced beauty of life itself.

In the Tarot, April is watched over by The Emperor card. Rather than a power-hungry vision of the patriarchy, this archetype is a reminder of our inherent birthright to be here in the first place. How do you enter a room? Do you shrink into smallness and fold into your body? Or puff out your chest, ready to do battle? The Emperor wants us to become seamlessly 'right-sized', taking up the space we naturally inhabit with no trace of either shrunken shame or inflated egoism.

Take this month to remember your upright animus – your very 'I am-ness'. Speak your name in front of the mirror. Look yourself straight in the eye and celebrate your personal contours, as you declare your aliveness like a just-born baby animal. Stage your own self-renewing ceremony that marries you to the essence of each present moment. When we let April's energy flow freely, we course through the world clad only in the fierce finery of our birthday suit, blood pumping with the notion that things can always be made simpler and more direct.

Endlessly regenerative, April is made for venerating any and every glimmer of newness and renewal in your life. Start with the cells turning over on the back of your hand. Or start with what's inside your kitchen cabinets. Start anywhere. Invent a language for each sensation and object that you see, and remake your world like a children's book of first words painted in primary shades.

There's still a chance for you to just be you, says April. You're here and you're alive and your very existence is where everything begins again. So get up, get out and get on with it.

APRIL DATES WITH DESTINY:
EMBRACE THE EASE

This month's magic comes from the doubled pleasure of two New Moons, the first in fire-starter Aries and the second, our first partial eclipse of the year, in chocolate box Taurus. This cosmic energy asks us to nourish ourselves with primary-coloured empowerment, embracing our fundamental rights to 'be' and to 'have'.

Use this month to **render your everyday existence more comfortable** – setting up your palace so that everything is bespoke, close at hand and good to go. How could you make your life easier? And what does the idea of 'ease' mean to you? Guilt? Boredom? Excitement? Whatever your attitude towards smoothing your way, let this month be an exploration of effortlessness – stocking the cabinets, simplifying the systems and swapping intricate buttons for some zippers and snaps.

New Moon in Aries

FIGHT FOR YOUR LIFE FORCE: The first New Moon of the astrological year, this bite-sized lunar happening is the boldest and the youngest of them all. Use this Moon phase to **return to innocence – considering what a less cynically seasoned version of you might say about a stuck situation.** A far cry from naivety, this is actually a moment to use all the bumps and bruises of the road you've already travelled to power you forwards. Rebrand your notion of friction, imagining that you're a fresh and eager boxer who uses your life force to fight *for* your right to be here, rather than *against* the forces you fear conspire to oppose you.

Venus enters Pisces

BELIEVE IN MAGIC: While Venus sometimes gets a reputation as all hearts-and-flowers romantic love, it is also the planet of pure dilation – opening us up towards the good stuff with trust and ease. In Pisces, our pleasure centre turns gauzy and glamorous, as we're beckoned to see the world through shimmery, soft-lit spectacles and **to believe the best of ourselves and others.** If taken to the extreme, this planetary transit can lead us to augment reality to fit our wildest whims. But life is hard, and most of us struggle with allowing ourselves to hope in the first place. So let this time be your ticket straight to dreamland, as you dare yourself to take a tumble in sweet imaginings of what could be.

Mercury enters Taurus
(enters Gemini on 29th)

BODY LANGUAGE: Mercury's metabolic functioning slows to a savoury flow as it enters Taurus, asking us to relish a little rumination and roll the possibilities in our mouths like a caramel candy. A powerful planetary transit of embodied knowing, Mercury in Taurus invites us **to trust in our sense of things.** Start by noticing where an idea or experience 'lands' in your body, staying with the physical sensation without having to chase the tail of the storyline itself. Come into communion with your body, attending to any subtle sensory cues and letting this be the first place you go for information about what is presenting in front of you.

Mars enters Pisces

DRIVEN BY THE DIVINE: On the surface, sensitive sea creature Pisces might appear to clash with the flashier ferocity of engine-revving Mars. Yet this transit is actually a rich opportunity for finding power in full presence – **a chance to sync our personal will with our larger soul 'moves'.** Start to explore this energy by noticing the different sorts of effort that live within you. Some kinds feel sexy, enlivening and exuberant. Some feel like chest-tightening anxiety that ultimately keeps us scrambling and small. Let this transit be an invitation to look at all the ways in which you power up, noticing when 'pushing' it creates push-back that just isn't worthy of your precious life force.

Full Moon in Libra

RESPOND TO THE REVERB: Sitting directly opposite Aries on the zodiac wheel, Libra energy is here to explore the 'effects' of the fire starter's 'cause'. This Full Moon is a magic moment for noticing the reverb of choices as they resound through your life. What paths have you taken and where have they led you? Rather than an excuse to engage in guilt-ridden talk of wrongdoing or a dead end that finds you trapped by former decisions, use this energy as a morning-after moment to simply take stock. You did what you could with where you were at every moment. Let this cosmic event enable you to **find forgiveness for all that you've been and done,** allowing this assessment to help you refine future reflexes.

Sun enters Taurus

TO HAVE AND TO HOLD: The transition from Aries to Taurus energy takes us from active, penetrative doing to the rich, rolling hills of receiving, as Aries' outpouring of energetic exuberance is omnivorously absorbed by the supple ground of Taurus. This cosmic changeover is a ripe opportunity to explore those instances when you push to produce through willpower and those others when you're able to 'hollow' and hold steady. **How do you 'take in' from life?** Whether it's your capacity to savour the swallow of a delicious beverage, or draw in a compliment without deflection, this solar shift wants you to make like a beautiful baguette and sop up every last drop of extra virgin olive oil.

Pluto stations retrograde in Capricorn
(until 8 October)

TRANSFORM YOUR TROPHIES: The higher-octave expression of the planet Mars, Pluto asks us to move beyond our personal mojo and get moved by life – revealing that where we hold on the hardest is precisely where we're being asked to let something die. It is in this letting go and composting process that we meet the eternal parts of ourselves that can never, ever be stolen. As Pluto slows its roll through Capricorn, we're invited to step into the belly of our self-sufficiency, paying attention to where we feel pressured to keep it all together. **What are you trying to hold up that just can't be supported any longer?** Take this time to release binary notions of triumph and competence, leaning into any fears about helplessness to let yourself be helped.

New Moon in Taurus
(partial solar eclipse)

THE COURAGE TO ENJOY IT: A New Moon for soothing any scarcity-driven survivalist fears, this astral event invites us to uncover the lusciousness of life – committing to the courageous act of enjoying whatever pleasures we find on our platters. **Even in the trickiest of moments, there exists some shred of sweetness,** and this extra-dark-chocolate cosmic event (with the Moon blocking much of the Sun's light) wants you to hunt it down and feast on it – amplifying your capacity for self-satisfaction. Whether it's a sudden spark of humour in the midst of a fight or a delicious breeze that carries your tears away with it, the Taurus New Moon beckons you to discover the hidden nectars of life.

STAR PARTY:
ECLIPSE SEASON PART ONE
(30 APRIL–16 MAY)

Cosmic blowouts of epic proportions that occur four
to six times per year, eclipses are wild occasions of
accelerated astrological soul growth. Taking place
on certain New Moons, solar eclipses ask for radical
beginnings, like trust falls, urging us to take leaps into
the unknown. And aligning with certain Full Moons, lunar
eclipses are culmination points that illuminate anything
we've been keeping in the shadows – inviting us to take
our fears for a final spin on the strobe-lit dance floor.
All eclipses travel in pairs of polarity point signs (two
signs opposite each other on the zodiac wheel),
and this year brings a no-holds-barred Taurus/
Scorpio party. Focused on desire, possession and
booty-shaking birth/death cycles, the first phase
of 2022 kicks off with the 30 April New Moon.
Igniting the plus-sized pleasure-seeking of Taurus,
it initiates a birthing time of abundant amplification,
as we learn to live and let live in all our largesse.

SIGN-BY-SIGN
GUIDE TO APRIL

♈ ARIES

Happy birthday season, baby burner! While your pulsing passion is sometimes painted as confrontational, any trace of combat is only evidence of your capacity to run at life full-throttle. This month, the cosmos wants you to use all that fierce force to become the co-creator of your world – as if you're a rapids-rafter or an open-kitchen chef, collaborating with the energies that rush to both meet and match you. How can you catch the natural current of right now, channelling the weather with arms lifted and head tilted back to greet the wild sky?

✦ With a Full Moon and a New Moon in Venus-ruled Libra and Taurus this month, it's prime time for considering your pliability and for choosing to partner with what's being magnetized to you. When you start to steel against a situation or feeling, practise relaxing your muscles instead, taking any resistance down and in like a fortifying snack. Far from rendering you more passive, this exercise in receptivity will expand your capacity for abundance and bolster your courage – if you allow it to.

♉ TAURUS

Two baby farm animals just learning to wander this brave new world, Taurus and Aries are here to savour immediate sensations and bright-eyed beginnings. Let April be your invitation to initiate – reaching out to grab the juicy fruits without having to wait for them to fall from the branch.

✦ With your ruler, Venus, travelling through dream-keeper Pisces, and a bonus New Moon in your sign at month's end, the world is yours for the treasuring. Embrace the ecstasy of embellishment without fear of being a little over the top.

♊ GEMINI

Gemini and Aries share a penchant for experiential learning and intrepid exploration. In April, you're invited to inject a little fine-tuned focus into your passion for remaining perpetually 'in process', as you make a beeline for what you desire.

✦ With your ruler, Mercury, transiting through the golden fields of Taurus on its way towards your sign, this April is an opportunity to see what 'sticks' – as you meld your usual mix-and-mingle energy with some solid grasps and held poses.

♋ CANCER

While your tucked-in seashell of sensitivity may sometimes feel challenged by all that hot-blooded Aries desert exposure, Cancer and Aries share a Cardinal capacity for initiation. April is an opportunity to embrace the 'charge' of your feelings, as you allow yourself to be motivated by whatever moves you.

✦ With all the Moon energy this month, you're sitting high on the pillow pile of your precious emotions. Let April be your chance to pour it on without pouting, as you let yourself get flooded with feeling and hold it all with grace.

♌ LEO

Leo and Aries share a gorgeous guilelessness, showing up with hearts on sleeves. Let this double dose of frankness help you simplify this month, allowing April to become a stripped-down party pack of only those gems that bedazzle you.

✦ As Saturn squares the North Node in fellow Fixed signs Aquarius and Taurus, it's time to get good and honest about the value of your rock-solid core. Tend to whatever tethers you, little love kitten, getting grounded as you gather your yarn back onto the ball.

♍ VIRGO

A complicated duet of integral operators, both Virgo and Aries venerate a bit of self-starting solitude. Let this April feel hermetically sealed, as you check in to your proverbial cabin in the woods without apology, only granting entry to who and what is most worthy of your company.

◆ As Mars enters your opposite sign of Pisces this month, you're asked to consider the sensitive subtlety of the choices you make, ensuring that each move aligns with every part of you, from the crown of your head to the tips of your toes.

♎ LIBRA

Facing off across an open field in the battle to balance willpower and compromise, both Libra and Aries contain the capacity for clear-eyed warriorship. April wants you to remember this fighting spirit and not to shy away from the fights that help refine your mission.

◆ With a Full Moon in your sign that gets extra juice from deep-diving Pluto, the month is ripe for staring straight into the eyes of whatever's right in front of you without blinking. A reckoning with reality is your golden ticket towards earth-shaking change.

♏ SCORPIO

Conjoined by your shared ancient ruler, Mars, both Scorpio and Aries are meaty magic-makers with hearty appetites to boot. Embrace a more straightforward flavour of ardour this month, as you follow the lead of uncomplicated cravings and make bold moves in broad daylight, snacking on whatever looks good.

✦ With your ruler, Pluto, poised to station retrograde at the end of this month, use April to consider the resources that have allowed you to weather every storm and to build solid faith in the pieces of you that are utterly unbreakable.

♐ SAGITTARIUS

Both bonfire babes who find pleasure in the burn, Sagittarius and Aries are hard-wired to trust in the luscious leaps of life. Take this month to learn a little bit from the leaner and more focused energy of Aries as you gather any far-flung sticks back to centre and keep the firepit consistently lit.

✦ With your ruler, Jupiter, making a charged visit to dream queen Neptune, let this month help you balance spread-eagled exploration by building a nest. Remember, the deeper your roots, the wilder your branches can become.

♑ CAPRICORN

Cardinal kids who love to be top of the class, Capricorn and Aries share an urge to get going and get ahead. This month is an opportunity to embrace a bit more of Aries' leap-before-you-look energy, forgoing some of your five-year plans for the sheer exhilaration of living in the moment.

✦ With Pluto enjoying its last pre-retrograde roll through your sign, use April to celebrate your personal history of transformation – considering all your incarnations and the serenity and strength you've uncovered in these shape-shifts.

♒ AQUARIUS

With a penchant for courageous contrarianism, both Aquarius and Aries aren't afraid of a little healthy exile in the name of innovation. Let April's Aries energy inject your polemics with more personal flair as you step out into the unknown, unafraid to back yourself on a bold stance – even when it might feel irrational.

✦ With guardian of the internal, eternal flame, the asteroid Vesta, making its inaugural full-month tour through your sign, devote yourself to keeping your creative cauldron lit by only bowing down to what matters most.

♓ PISCES

Celestial neighbours on the zodiac wheel, Pisces and Aries are both learning to share the sugar when needed. This month, you're asked to borrow some of Aries' spice to balance out your sweetness. Embrace your more intense emotions and allow the boldness that comes with this to power up your ability to stand on your own two feet.

✦ With Venus and Mars rocketing through your sign this month, it's a moment for amorous self-advocacy. Define your own 'desire diet', eschewing external input about what's best for you and following your most carnal cravings.

STAR STYLE

COLOUR: Draw design inspo from indoor–outdoor shades, just-born hues and game-room primaries like sparkling whites, ripe and ready bright greens and sunny reds and oranges.

A

FASHION: Try on rugged, kinetic looks that walk the line between in-your-face antics and innocent minimalism, with cotton tees, high-waisted blue jeans, slim-fitting motorcycle jackets, disco jumpsuits, low-heeled boots, no-nonsense short nails and ponytails. Experiment with finding your 'uniform', simplifying your routine with a power ensemble that lets you move with ease.

SCENT: April's aromas are clean, direct and spicy-sweet, like cedarwood, classic *fougère* fragrances, baby powder, shower gel, freshly cut grass, dirt and matches.

FOOD FOR THE SOUL

April's flavours feel good as they burn. Try chilli-pepper dark chocolate, Red Hots cinnamon candy, and sweet and smoky mesquite on your barbecue. Partner this self-expressive spiciness with shallots, frittatas and the pared-down farm freshness of sheep's milk ice cream.

CHART YOUR COURSE

April's energies activate our urge to stake our flags in fresh ground. Explore your readiness to try out a brand new world with a solo visit to brazenly innovative New York City, brashly big-hatted Texas or the Australian Outback. Closer to home, make bold forays into unfamiliar neighbourhoods, forge self-led trails through the woods and even practise staying in one place – committing to standing upright on your personal patch of earth, exactly where you are, as you are.

ELEMENTAL EXCURSIONS

Cardinal Fire sign-ruled April is made for fierce frictional fun and springing into action. Think salsa dancing, capoeira, blind dates, new haircuts, finger-painting, fast cars, single-pointed focus, starting lines and self-directed struts through city streets to a soundtrack all your own.

PLANETARY PROMPTS

Use these magic words and journal
questions to moor you this month...

INNOCENCE:

How can I simplify my life and what is the
'heart' of each matter that arises?

SPARK:

How do I 'power up' and get my blood pumping?

INITIATION:

Where can I just say 'yes' and how can
I support this bold beginning?

LIFE FORCE:

What is my relationship to conflict and
what am I ready to fight for?

BIRTHRIGHT:

What brings me most fully alive?

A

MONDAY	TUESDAY	WEDNESDAY	THURSDAY	FRIDAY	SATURDAY	SUNDAY
2 MAY Venus enters Aries						
	10 MAY Mercury stations retrograde in Gemini + Jupiter enters Aries					
16 MAY Full Moon in Scorpio (total lunar eclipse)					**21 MAY** Sun enters Gemini	
	24 MAY Mars enters Aries					
30 MAY New Moon in Gemini						

MAY

THE PLEASURE
IS ALL YOURS

THE PLEASURE
IS ALL YOURS

Redolent of ripe rose petals and buttered up for the buffet, May's astrology is filled to the full-bodied brim – a richly perfumed invite from the cosmos to claim our plus-sized pleasure chest without apology.

This lushly lubed-up month is led by the second sign of Taurus – the zodiac's abundant bounty bundle that just keeps on blooming. Pause to turn the sound of this sign over in your mouth for a moment, conjuring images of Roman banquets and luxuriously laden grapevines. The Sun arrived in the Earth sign energy of Taurus in late April and it's time to enjoy it, making May a month to touch, taste, smell and relish. Roll in it, celebrating the hothouse hedonism of our right to have and to hold.

A call to feast fully at the farmhouse table, it's a month for making peace with our appetites – learning to want whatever feels good to want and to reach for more, more and yet more of it. In the process, we're asked to build tangible trust in the strong and steady self-renewing cornucopia contained within.

Take this time to bolster your belief that you deserve to desire exactly what you desire and to tend to anxious fears of unworthiness or too-muchness, or unfounded anticipation of the moments when it all might be taken away. Life tastes even sweeter when powered by a self-fulfilled sense of full-up-ness, where all the rest is delicious icing on the already good-enough cake.

In the Tarot, May is hosted by The Empress card – a decadent dilator of deservedness that opens our legs and parts our lips so that life can love us more lustrously. The Empress saturates us in sensation, each feeling tone a flavour that's worth savouring. No matter our libidinous proclivities, at its heart and soul, this month wants to be let in and drunk down, without us wasting one precious drop.

A ripe reward for April's jacked-up striving, May slows our roll and shows us how to magnetize what we want, as we make like the cacao-coated earth beneath us, absorbing whatever fertile fuel comes our way. Far from passive, this process actually invites us to say 'yes' to our human part in the planetary cycles, and to come back to our organic roots. Look around. Sniff the air. Taste the sunshine on your tongue and tune into your bodily pleasure centres. How can you make your life a V-shaped valley that covets and cherishes whatever it catches?

It is time to slip into something much more comfortable and relish your right to move through the world with radiant ease. May serves everything up on a lickable silver spoon – reminding us that the so-called 'simple' life is actually made from the very best stuff on Earth.

MAY DATES WITH DESTINY:
PRISMATIC POSSIBILITY

This month is a cosmic takeout container popping with rainbow confetti, as a pack of planets races through Aries. Accompanied by the year's second Mercury retrograde in the planet's winged home sign of Gemini, and a raw and revelatory total lunar eclipse in Scorpio, transformation is afoot. How to ride with the times? **Remain ready to be surprised and get curious about the cracks where the light gets in.**

In the Tarot, this is Eight of Swords energy, a card that appears to present 'no way out' until we notice that the feet of the figure represented on the card remain free to walk away. Take this month to notice where your mind wants to swirl and spin like a lazy laundry cycle, stuck in the 'same old, same old', and then pay attention to the almost imperceptible new soap bubbles that are rising to the surface. Fresh ideas are worth pursuing, so give some extra love to any new butterflies that are hand-delivering alternate options on their wunderkind wings.

Venus enters Aries

(enters Taurus on 28th)

THE HEART WANTS WHAT IT WANTS: Venus, the pleasure planet of dilated desire, is in its 'detriment' in Aries, indicating that while it may not appear comfy on the surface, its gifts can be uncovered by pushing beyond the status quo. In contrast to Venus' usual 'wait and receive' factory setting, this journey through the first of the Fire signs activates our magnetism, giving us **the courage to make a beeline for whatever bounty we crave**. Take this transit to actively assert your appetites, noticing when you feel the need to secretly indulge a 'guilty pleasure' instead of just inviting it to the breakfast table. A prime time to bring any secret loves out of hiding and kiss them in the morning light. Once Venus hits home turf in Taurus on the 28th, we can rest on our laurels and lick the spoon.

Mercury stations retrograde in Gemini

(enters Taurus on 23rd; stations direct in Taurus on 3rd June)

BREATHING PATTERNS: Naturally ruling over the sign of Gemini, Mercury is what gives the sign its breathiness and levity. Any passage of this planet through Gemini's rainbowed prism reminds us to pay attention to life's micro magic moments, noticing how our perceptions shift with every tiny tweak to our environment. With the second Mercury retrograde of the year in effect, we're given another chance to edit our story – choosing which tales we'd like to keep telling ourselves and which plotlines are ready to be purged. In Gemini, the focus is on our literal and metaphorical respirations. **Begin by simply paying attention to your breath: what is the ratio of inhale to exhale?** If you're holding it in, maybe it's time to linger a little on the outbreaths, relaxing into sharing more of yourself with the world. If it's the opposite, take this time to fill your lungs, as you learn to take more in without racing to put out.

Jupiter enters Aries

FIND YOUR EDGE: As larger-than-life Jupiter begins its nearly two-year roll through Aries (though it'll retrograde back into Pisces in October–December), we're asked to explore the energy of risk in all its daring incarnations. Before you immediately force yourself out of the plane with no parachute, **start by sidling up to your 'edge' in subtler ways.** Notice the point in partnership when you suddenly want to cut and run. Or the moment in a meeting where you long to speak up but stifle the urge. This planetary transit takes off the handbrake, asking us to ease ourselves out of the comfort zone of sneakers and sweats and into our aerodynamic skydiving suits.

Full Moon in Scorpio
(total lunar eclipse)

THE NATURE OF THE BEAST: The down-and-dirty root systems that lie beneath the earth of Taurus' perfumed blooms, Scorpio energy forces us to face the muck that feeds the flowers. With the Earth's shadow intensifying the light of the Full Moon, expect this lunar cycle to unleash all aspects of your nature – as you're asked to **take a long hard look at your patterns and proclivities without leaving a single stone unturned**. Notice where you start to split your personal qualities into pros and cons, prizing certain parts of yourself and relegating others to a dusty casket under the bed. When you come across a quality that makes you queasy, sit with it and ask it what it wants. What are its deepest longings? Its hopes and dreams? What is it trying to achieve? Look to nature itself for inspiration: animals don't judge themselves for who and what they are – they simply evolve their behaviour to best serve their survival.

Sun enters Gemini

STREET SMARTS: The Sun's transition from Taurus to Gemini invites us to push back from our seats at the banquet and head out for some street-cart eats. Let this passing of the zodiacal baton help you

find a balance between going with what you know and coming gloriously unglued, as you explore the relationship between comfort and curiosity. Which parts of your life are ready for some fresh air? And how can you hold yourself steady as you step out, so you don't lose your centre with the slightest breeze or bump in the road? This transition wants us to mix inside with outside and to find our internal anchors even when we're freewheeling through the fray.

Mars enters Aries

FUN WITH FRICTION: As Mars returns home to its original source of life force, Aries, the power moves start to pump and pulsate. Take this transit to **consider your relationship to friction, noticing how your system ignites in the face of a perceived challenge or rough edge.** Has life led you to believe that the only way to make things happen is to hunt them down and force them to bend to your will? Or do you tend to go limp in the face of adversity, fearing that standing up for yourself will turn the world against you? Let this transit help you explore new ways of asserting yourself as you learn to use your quickening pulse in service of your most vivid and vital desires.

30

New Moon in Gemini

MOOD RING MAGIC: A multi-faceted moment for making love to all our angles, this Mutable Gemini Moon wants to remind us that **feeling is not always fact.** Start by steeping yourself in whatever emotional flux is arising before detaching from the feeling and engaging in some friendly observation. How long does each sensation last? When and how do some get stuck while others quickly fly away? And how does your mind manipulate and extend the mega-mix, giving extra airtime to certain feeling states? Continue the questioning throughout the coming New Moon phase, as this open-ended exploration helps you sample new ways of engaging with your emotions.

M

STAR PARTY:
BELTANE (1 MAY)

The second cross-quarter holiday on the Pagan Wheel of the Year, Beltane, or May Day, bursts with bonfires and bouquets and is a festival that traditionally celebrated the full flower and fecundity of spring. A time for strong and steady space-holding, Beltane's rituals included building hearty hearths and drawing water from holy wells. Let this energy grant you the unapologetic permission to fortify your own fount this May, as you tend to the flora and fauna of your inner and outer gardens.

SIGN-BY-SIGN
GUIDE TO MAY

♉ TAURUS

Happy birth time, beauteous bombshell! While your sign sometimes gets a rep for being staid or stubborn, with the Sun coaxing you out of your den, May is a month for divining where and how you can open your petals to accept more delicious dew. Start with a simple exercise in orientation. Which parts of your life feel sealed up? Which parts are begging to be unfolded and adored? Let May be your moment to strike a balance between weatherproofing your metaphorical abode and throwing open the French doors to the sun.

✦ With your ruler, Venus, travelling through Aries' courageous, cinnamon-scented country alongside Mars, take this time to consider your relationship with the notion of give-and-take. Smoke out any stories of martyrdom, and focus on a no-nonsense equation of empty and full. The maths might be easier than you think: when you've got extra resources on hand, spill the bounty; and when you're feeling depleted, pause to restock the fridge.

♊ GEMINI

Here to savour the shiny sensations of life on earth, both Gemini and Taurus are wide-eyed kids in the ice-cream shop. Take May to remember that you, too, are the purveyor of all this sweetness. Notice when you're waiting to be served by the world, and adopt a more actively creative role in delivering the goodies.

✦ With your ruler, Mercury, travelling retrograde through Taurus and meeting up with desirous Mars and Pluto, it's a month to back your intuition and instincts with action, as you reclaim the right to your own self-actualization.

♋ CANCER

Both Cancer and Taurus receive with arms wide open, surrounding and incubating life's tender moments with their fiercely feathered nests. Take May to consider the padlocks you place on that which you covet and cherish, and see if you can learn to crack open the lid without fearing you'll lose the love.

✦ This month's Moon cycle mixes Water and Air, and asks you to embrace the expansive ambiguity of your feelings. Follow any tingles and trails of tears all the way back to where they came from, to uncover what truly moves you.

♌ LEO

Here for Fixed-sign fun, both Leo and Taurus immerse themselves in the immediacy of unapologetic enjoyment. Let May be your invitation to revel in the oversized joys of whatever pleasures are close at hand, as you romance the right here, right now.

✦ With bountiful Jupiter entering fellow Fire sign Aries, May is made for indulging in a little healthy drama, complete with buttered popcorn. Follow through on any intense urges cleanly and without apology and enjoy the sensation of spilling over the top.

♍ VIRGO

With their feet firmly on the ground, Virgo and Taurus both find magic in the mundane and the material. Let May remind you that what's yours will always be yours, and that you never have to 'make good' to be more than good enough.

✦ As your ruler, Mercury, meets up with Jupiter this month, it's time to let out a long and longed-for sigh of relief. Where can you allow yourself an outbreath on an issue that's been bothering you – dropping your to-do list and letting unseen forces sort it out in the back room on your behalf?

♎ LIBRA

Dually ruled by queen of the silk sheets Venus, both Libra and Taurus are here to elevate the art of living well. Take some lessons from the earthier inclinations of Taurus this month, noticing when your urge to refine could be swapped for relishing the already perfect taste of sugar in the raw.

◆ With Venus and Mars joining forces in your polarity point sign of Aries, the invitation this month is to own your own enjoyment. Consider and notice where you can practise 'going first' – revealing what you want without waiting for someone else to ask.

♏ SCORPIO

Forming an oppositional axis in the zodiac wheel, both Scorpio and Taurus are on a mission to explore our human urges to have and to hold. Take May to reincarnate into your original animal skin and to relish a roll in the hay. Whatever you find yourself wanting right now is absolutely right.

◆ With a Full Moon lunar eclipse in your sign mid-month, May is made for harvesting your ripest grapes. See whatever is coming close to completion in your life as having reached its capacity for growth. Rather than a burn-it-down-to-the-ground ending, what would feel like a fitting celebration of this particular life cycle?

♐ SAGITTARIUS

On the surface, Taurus energy may seem too limiting for your adventurous nature, but this Fixed Earth sign shares the wild Sagittarian trust in following your instinctual nature. Use May to commit to your natural inner laws and to construct your own fences instead of feeling penned in or put upon by the constraints of others.

✦ With your ruler, Jupiter, shifting gears into fellow Fire sign Aries this month, it's time to power up with a sense of personal ownership. Transition from party guest to host, as you practise taking greater control of the ambience of your existence.

♑ CAPRICORN

From uncut geode to 24-carat jewel, both Capricorn and Taurus turn the raw matter of life into utter luxury. Let May be your invitation to trust once again in the ground beneath your feet, as you steady your hooves on whatever mountain you are currently climbing.

◆ With a pack of go-getter planets in Aries goading your sign this month, it's a time for sussing out which of your self-imposed limits is no longer serving you. Keep your pencil eraser handy for getting rid of any lines that are beginning to feel like too-hard boundaries.

♒ AQUARIUS

Two Fixed signs on the journey to make peace with your nature and nature itself, both Aquarius and Taurus are in a dance to divine exactly the right moment to make moves. May is your reminder that staying in touch with your surroundings will spark transformations that are truly aligned with your soul.

◆ With this month's emphasis on the fledglings of the zodiac, Aries, Taurus and Gemini, you're asked to consider your own relationship to innocence. Where could you 'grow down', embracing an earlier, less weathered and more optimistic version of you?

♓ PISCES

While earthy Taurus may initially seem to challenge your ethereal eccentricities, both Pisces and Taurus long to be tended to by the world around them. Use May to remember that you are the arbiter of your own enjoyment and that you can always meet your own material world needs.

✦ As the astrological year shifts into high gear, take time to tend to your internal experience amid these more forceful energies of exposure. Consciously choose parts of you to keep safely hidden, held in your heart-shaped locket for your eyes only.

♈ ARIES

The original dynamic duo that leads the rest of the astro pack, both Aries and Taurus are like just-born babes who've landed on Earth to give it their best shot. Make May your moment for out-of-the-eggshell exploration, Aries, as you acknowledge when you've gone astray and find the strength to start again.

✦ With Venus, Mars and Jupiter all entering your sign, your boldest burners are lustrously lit. Soothe any anxiety that comes with this abundance of gotta-have-it energy by keeping expectations about how you'll go about it loose.

STAR STYLE

COLOUR: Revel in the rustic delights of country living and romps through the lush leafy highlands with chocolate-box tints of cream, caramel and pale pink, paired with pure gold and verdant greens.

FASHION: Slip into beautifully basic, comfortable luxury that moulds to the body like a second skin. Think silk blouses, bombastic medallions, worn-in leather, voluminous *Dallas*-style hairdos, emerald accents, studded belts, lavish lingerie. Whatever your style, let your threads celebrate every inch of your body.

SCENT: May's aromas are opulently overripe, full-bodied florals. Think tuberose and peony, sweet blond tobacco, musk, leather and coumarin accords (a warming, caramelized fragrance blend smelling of herbs and almonds).

FOOD FOR THE SOUL

Treat yourself with headily hedonistic and richly robust tastes, like truffles, drinking chocolate, mulled wine, dark cherries, slow roasts, high-quality olive oil and creamy burrata or Saint André cheese.

CHART YOUR COURSE

May's energies awaken our inherent love affair with Earth. Soak it all up, with visits to verdant valleys, meadows and lush farmlands, Mediterranean locales that emphasize ample siestas and epic dinners, and all-inclusive vacations where everything is plentifully provided. Closer to home, book your favourite table at a beloved restaurant you usually save for special occasions, snuggle down in a comfy chair in your own abode, or spend a whole day in bed.

ELEMENTAL EXCURSIONS

Fixed Earth-sign-ruled May is made for the down-to-earth and grounded sensory stability that supports the soul. Think botanical gardens, buffet brunches, rolls in the hay, horseback riding, lovemaking, sofa time and laying your body directly on the ground as you learn to put your faith in the planet's endless provisions.

PLANETARY PROMPTS

Use these magic words and journal
questions to moor you this month...

WORTH:

How can I build trust that what is meant
for me is coming my way?

SENSUALITY:

How can I bring each of my five senses alive and
what messages is my body sending me?

EASE:

What creature comforts can help sweeten things?

RECEIVING:

Where am I being asked to widen and 'take in' from life?

NATURE:

Which core personal qualities anchor
me in moments of flux?

M

MONDAY	TUESDAY	WEDNESDAY	THURSDAY	FRIDAY	SATURDAY	SUNDAY
				3 JUNE Mercury stations direct in Taurus	**4 JUNE** Saturn stations retrograde in Aquarius	
	14 JUNE Full Moon in Sagittarius					
	21 JUNE Sun enters Cancer		**23 JUNE** Venus enters Gemini			
	28 JUNE Neptune stations retrograde in Pisces	**29 JUNE** New Moon in Cancer				

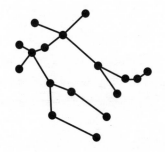

JUNE

INHABIT THE
IN-BETWEEN

INHABIT THE
IN-BETWEEN

A symphony of shimmers that catch the light and refract its rainbow, June's astrology is synchronized and serendipitous – a chance to pay attention to each prismatic particle of stardust that meets the eye.

These sensations ride on the wings of Gemini, the third sign – a sneakered and backpacked cosmic kid, who's eager to learn from the school of life. June's energy wants us to grow as we go, apprenticing ourselves to the process with pencils at the ready, as we joyously adopt the credo that we don't ever really 'know' anything. Let ambiguity be your ally this month, freeing the vines of your mind from the confines of 'either/or' to reach out towards the multi-faceted land of 'both/and'.

Start by noticing any binary thinking that's limiting your world view, making you rush to categorize or draw conclusions by pigeonholing phenomena into a 'this' or 'that' slot. What fuels this kind of thinking? Do you believe that hard lines and limitations will keep everything in its place and safe from harm?

June urges us to swap any stagnant life geometry for a more liminal limbo, letting our beliefs become both translucent and untranslatable – touched by the changing light and full of infinite potential meanings.

June's Mutable Air sign messages are present in every butterfly breath we take, a reminder that we are active participants in a dance of eternal, ethereal exchange. What nearly imperceptible imprints are you leaving as you walk to the shops or smile at a stranger? And what love notes await you around every corner when you pay closer attention to the cracks in the pavement? Let yourself and everything that surrounds you become mutual muses this month, following the traces of what inspires you, and leaving a trail of creative crumbs in your wake.

In the Tarot, June's Gemini energy gets its creatrix-charge from The Magician card. A channel of inspiration and activation, this archetype asks us to attend to our open-and-shut flaps, as we balance opening to catch inspiration on our palms with the ability to seal up and bring something into being that's all our own. Think of this month as your adaptive and infinite opportunity to become a conduit for whatever wants to reach you.

June invites us to listen to the language that animates the world's woodwork when we think everything is asleep; the whispered cosmic communiqués that have room to reach us when we move beyond obvious explanations. Take this month to commit to the chameleon opportunity to choose your own adventure, breaking the brittleness of certainty in two and tasting every shade of the rainbow.

JUNE DATES WITH DESTINY: WEIGH YOUR OPTIONS

June sees light-footed Mercury stationing direct, gravity-laden Saturn stationing retrograde and some of the zodiac's most fantastical friends (Gemini, Sagittarius and Cancer) hosting the party. This makes the month an exercise in understanding our relationship to the forces that bind us and also to our utter boundlessness.

If that sounds far out, **start with a straightforward check-in about which areas of your life feel 'heavy' and which feel 'light'.** For the heavy parts, what are the qualities of weight? Does a particular partnership or project feel dense because it's just hard work? Does it bring up heavy emotions that feel like they are flattening you? Or is the weight of it strengthening, asking you to muscle up when the going gets tough? Likewise, are the lighter parts delightfully winged invites to loosen your hold? Or distracting 'flyaways' that you are ready to free yourself from? Assess the relative heft of each of your endeavours and find your ideal load by balancing getting grounded with letting go.

Mercury stations direct in Taurus
(re-enters Gemini on 13th)

MAGNETIC MOVEMENT: With Mercury doing a tango between Taurus and Gemini since mid-April, this final direct dance back towards its home sign quickens the metabolism of life, allowing us to put May's careful calibration into action. Take this transit to **consider the naturally regulating in-out energies of your life** and commit to really tuning in to these cycles and following their lead. When something reaches its maximum capacity, it starts to spill over. And when something is empty, there's room to fill up. Treat yourself like a magic magnet that moves instinctively towards and away from the charge it needs, without getting caught in the meaning of each interaction.

Saturn stations retrograde in Aquarius
(until 23 October)

BREAK THE BOXES: As heavy-hitting Saturn slows down in spacious Aquarius, **interrogate where compartmentalizing your life is causing constriction**. Start by taking a look at which parts of yourself you 'leave out' as you adopt certain roles. Maybe it's something you secretly enjoy that you keep from a close friend, believing that they just wouldn't understand. Or an insecurity you cover up at work because you think sharing it would make you appear less competent. This planetary transit is made for breaking the boundaries of your inner bento box and committing to the radical belief that sharing all your pieces can profoundly contribute to the world.

Full Moon in Sagittarius

THE WILDS WITHIN: An unbridled Moon for spilling over the top and out across the open plains, this lunar event asks us to consider our own brand of wildness. While the word 'wild' can conjure up images of hard-partying extroverts and freewheeling spontaneity, this concept can be applied to any kind of intuitive movement. Look to nature for inspiration, as you notice how each animal and plant follows its own eternal expansion process through cell division over its particular life span. Take this Full Moon to consider when you could challenge an external rubric that tells you where you 'should' be headed and when to prune your progress, and **commit instead to following the lead of the bespoke blueprint for personal growth that exists inside you.**

Sun enters Cancer

REACH OUT FROM THE INSIDE: The Sun's transition from Gemini to Cancer energy is a conch-shell call to balance our 'up-and-out' circulation with some 'down-and-in' rejuvenation. Let this changing of the cosmic guard bring you into communion with your personal tidal pulls, and continue to examine any assumptions about how you think your growth pattern should unfold. **Are you waiting for that perfect job, partner or external push to provoke a shift?** Take this time to change gears, as you begin to allow a deep-sea exploration and expansion of your inner coves to catalyse the external waves you crave.

Venus enters Gemini

WHAT YOU SEEK IS SEEKING YOU: Through its association with The Lovers card in the Tarot, Gemini has a special relationship with Venus energy. This annual planetary passage encourages us to remember that everything we sweetly reach towards in the world wants to send our honey boomeranging back into our own beehive. Consider a quality you admire in a friend, or a colour you delight in seeing painted on a wall. While it may sound strange, that wall *wants* your gaze upon it, and the very quality you so appreciate is activated in you through the act of admiration. Let this transit be a time to **notice and love-up on what you love, as you invite it back to you.**

Neptune stations retrograde in Pisces
(until 4 December)

A FANTASY SUITE: As the misty mystic Neptune readies for a retrograde turn, this transit asks you to **consider your relationship to the tender process of wishing, hoping and bringing your fantasies down to earth.** Begin by noticing any feelings of emptiness in your dreaming, attending to where you might be waiting for your saviour in white satin to arrive, bearing your happiness on a silver platter. Whipped-cream dreams that become cake we can actually eat are made from equal parts imagination and elbow grease, and this transit asks us to bring conscious commitment to forging our fantasies, instead of simply waiting to magically catch their drift.

New Moon in Cancer

BEGIN AT THE BEGINNING: Coming just after the solstice, this salt-soaked Moon is one of the most tender and loony lunar happenings of the year, finding its feathered nest in its home sign of Cancer.

Watching over our most protected places, Cancerian energy invites us to swirl back towards the rooted base of our beings, as we tend to our emotional history and family inheritance. Take this New Moon phase to **give extra special attention to any feelings that play on repeat, exploring their origins** and finding freedom in the fact that you actually get to respond however you want. When we commit to listening to the elements of our past lives that echo in the present, we realize we don't have to 'carry' it all any longer.

J

STAR PARTY:
SOLSTICE (21 JUNE)

Occurring on the 21st, the longest day of the year in the
northern hemisphere and the shortest in the southern
hemisphere, the summer or winter solstice asks us to
interrogate the very bedrock on which our lives are
built. (The other solstice occurs on 21 December.) In
astrology, the summer and winter solstices activate the
axis of Cancer–Capricorn, signs that are here to help
us shape our notions of home and to create emotional
and material security to shelter us from life's storms.
At this solstice on 21 June, the Cancer end of the axis
comes into play. Think of this time as your chance
to consider the skin of your energetic security and
take stock of your bunkers, divining the difference
between hiding out and finding holy high ground.

SIGN-BY-SIGN
GUIDE TO JUNE

♊ GEMINI

Happy birth month, winged wonder! June is your time to revel in your unique brand of mix-and-match magic, celebrating your shimmering status as a creative channel. Tune in to the subtlest signals and notice when an idea bubbles up or a feeling starts to change. These threshold-crossing moments are when your precious porousness begins to dilate, readying itself to let in new life. You don't have to choose or commit to anything hard and fast. Trust that when you stay soft and simply let it all pass through, you'll catch on the tip of your tongue whatever precious particles are meant for you.

✦ With the astro energy of June asking us to challenge the notion of compartmentalization, it's a month to pay attention to some of the means by which you 'fly away' from certain feelings – sending them up and out to a headier mental realm before they're allowed to inhabit the heart and body. Rather than letting them cause self-critique, just turn your curiosity here, noticing how you categorize sensations and how some might be longing for a little more of your attention before they're sent away.

♋ CANCER

While Gemini is all mental buzz to your emo oceanic waves, Cancer shares its rainbow rhythm of catch and release, deciding what to bring into your shell and what to toss to the high seas. Have some fun with filtration during June, playing with what and who you let in and leave out through a process of pick 'n' mix.

♦ As June's New and Full Moons beckon you towards the wide-open plains of Sagittarius country, it's a month to make like a hermit crab and strap your house to your back. No matter what changes are afoot, think about how you can find inroads towards internal sanctuary, even when you're far from your home base.

♌ LEO

Leo and Gemini are the lovers of the zodiac – both perpetually party-ready to be dazzled by life's buffet. In June, how about allowing the world to show itself to you before you put on a song and dance? It's a time to find an outbreath in a bit of healthy 'invisibility', as you watch the wild unfolding without having to control the lighting.

♦ With Saturn stationing retrograde in your opposite sign of Aquarius, this month asks you to consider your motivations behind any urges to share of yourself. Pay attention to when this feels like glamorous generosity and when there's a secret 'get' behind an act of giving.

♍ VIRGO

Ruled by light-footed Mercury, both Virgo and Gemini have highly active nervous systems and nimble fingers that love to tweak and tailor the world around them. This month, borrow a bit of Gemini's butterfly buzz to let it all just pass through you, honing your capacity to ride the shifting ground and noticing how no single sensation sticks around for long.

✦ As Neptune stations retrograde in your polar sign of Pisces, you're invited to take up residence in the land of the seemingly impossible. Notice when you put the lid on a potential option before it has the chance to take seed, and commit to claiming your right to infinite choice.

♎ LIBRA

Forever rotating the crystals in search of reflective clarity, both Libra and Gemini are here to dance in life's light show. This month, take a page out of Gemini's choose-your-own-adventure novel, finding comfort in the land beyond either/or. Trust that you don't have to get it 'right' straight away; a step in any direction opens doors.

✦ With your fellow Air signs Aquarius and Gemini both being activated this month, play with your capacity to create change by shifting concepts and gears. Power up by imagining yourself in best-case scenarios and seeking the detours to take you there.

♏ SCORPIO

The magic string that pulls you out of your underground bunker, Gemini's energy helps you catch your breath and hover for a moment. In June you're invited to drop the effort, as you adopt a lighter touch. What you're truly meant to possess will boomerang back of its own accord.

◆ With your two honorary rulers, revved-up Mars and the untameable Lilith, facing off this month, June asks you to consider exactly what you're defending so hard. What do you believe you would lose if you let down your guard, and why is this not true?

♐ SAGITTARIUS

Sitting opposite Sagittarius in the zodiac wheel, Gemini is the baby-animal apprentice gathering on-the-ground intel to channel into your master suite of higher meaning. Consider June as back-to-school time, questioning any place you think you already know it all. Get comfy with uncertainty, hit the streets and let yourself get a little bit lost.

✦ With this month's Full Moon in your sign getting extra juice from Saturn and Neptune, it's time to break it down to build it back up. Notice what's naturally ready to dissolve and let the floorboards fall away to become kindling for a new plan.

♑ CAPRICORN

The butterfly to your truffle butter, Gemini energy infuses Capricorn's hard-won, high-quality efforts with a little evanescence. Take June to consider ways to become unbuttoned. Whether it's leaving a superfluous task temporarily undone or learning to let a project evolve through critique, it's a month to find levity in tossing the tangible to the sky.

✦ As your ruler, Saturn, starts its retrograde roll through Aquarius, this month is an opportunity for excavating and consciously creating internal space. Give yourself the gift of time, soothing any rushed need to 'prove' something in service of a rhythm more worthy of your regal nature.

♒ AQUARIUS

The ground control to your outer-space voyage, Gemini energy invigorates panned-out Aquarian prophecies with a joyous dip into the palette of possible outcomes. Take June to remember that your visions don't have to be in service of any endgame right now, and to allow yourself to find magic in messing around and trying it all on.

✦ As Saturn stations retrograde in your sign, you're invited to tend the tender places you believe must be fixed for you to be 'fit'. Your very humanness is the gateway to your divinity; let each gap in your story compassionately crack you open.

♓ PISCES

Fairy-like figures who drift and glide through life, both Pisces and Gemini are sensitive anemones, gathering up glitter as they go. This month, remember that you make an effect on your environment, too – touching in with how a change in your own internal weather might better fertilize and nurture the crops that surround you.

✦ With your ruler, Neptune, stationing retrograde, consider where you are shutting your eyes and awaiting a magic fix to a perceived problem. Look it right in the eye to create lasting alterations this month; cast your spells from a place of utter clarity.

♈ ARIES

Street-smart spark plugs who find courage in curiously colliding with the world, both Aries and Gemini are here to enter life at ground level and learn on the go. Let June be an invitation to balance big leaps with the art of packing for the ride, as you prepare yourself to engage with each part of the process.

✦ As your ruler, Mars, meets up with Saturn, Chiron and the lunar point Lilith, examine where you may be taking an overly aggressive stance. Is any of your flexing actually based in fear? Press pause on power moves that are purely a reaction against perceived powerlessness.

♉ TAURUS

The reiki to your deep-tissue massage, Gemini energy teaches Taurus to touch in with life's more subtle pleasures, helping you delight in whatever alights on your shoulder without having to grasp it. Let June be your invitation to find presence in the ephemeral, treating each magic moment like a luscious last supper.

✦ As your ruler, Venus, floats into Gemini, let this month be your personal pleasure chest – allowing whatever turns you on to guide you back towards what you know will always be yours. Notice how even something as seemingly simple as a favourite colour can reveal the core values you hold dearest.

STAR STYLE

COLOUR: Slip somewhere over the rainbow with iridescence, parakeet green, bumblebee topaz, citrine glitter flecks, diaphanous blue butterfly wings, mood ring swirls and prisms that crack you open to multiple perspectives.

FASHION: Draw inspo from an imaginary meet-up between street-smart androgyny, ethereal glitter rock and high-low cultural collisions. Think feathers, gossamer, multicoloured high tops, sparkly backpacks, delirious prints, plastic bangles and snap-on bracelets. Whatever your outfit, let your threads be extra-breathable, movable and mix-and-matchable to allow you to change your look with on-the-go ease.

SCENT: June's aromas are youthful and dazzlingly disorienting mixtures of synthetic and organic, which both excite and confuse our olfactory sensibilities. Think cyclamen, marjoram, Thierry Mugler's ecstatically strange 'Angel' perfume, or the whiff of a stranger's cologne that you catch out on the street.

FOOD FOR THE SOUL

Sample cheekily youthful and varied flavours and unexpected snacks, like nasturtium salads, tapas and mezze platters, ice-cream sundaes, bags of sweets, street-cart eats and bodega treats.

CHART YOUR COURSE

June's energies find us wandering the streets with our feelers friskily unfurled. Delight in the cacophonous circulation of any labyrinthine city, especially those that are equal parts urban mecca and interconnected villages, like San Francisco, Amsterdam and Melbourne. Closer to home, commit to exploring a new neighbourhood or outdoor market in your town, chatting to strangers on the bus and smiling at passers-by. Or simply knock on your next-door neighbour's door and ask to borrow some butter.

ELEMENTAL EXCURSIONS

Mutable Air-sign-ruled June is built for light-footed encounters and mind-altering mix-and-matches. Think flea markets and bazaars, walking tours and scavenger hunts, word games and puzzles, DJ parties, letter-writing, subscription boxes, bicycle rides, epic phone chats and clothing swaps.

PLANETARY PROMPTS

Use these magic words and journal
questions to moor you this month…

ATTUNEMENT:

What's my current balance between uptake
and output, and where might my nervous
system need some recalibration?

CHANNELLING:

How does inspiration reach me?

CURIOSITY:

How can I practise staying open to life's surprises?

IN-BETWEEN:

What thresholds am I crossing, and how can I
support myself in these transitional spaces?

ADAPTATION:

Where might I swap an 'either/or'
perspective for a 'both/and'?

J

MONDAY	TUESDAY	WEDNESDAY	THURSDAY	FRIDAY	SATURDAY	SUNDAY
	5 JULY Mercury enters Cancer + Mars enters Taurus					
		13 JULY Full Moon in Capricorn				
18 JULY Venus enters Cancer	**19 JULY** Chiron stations retrograde in Aries			**22 JULY** Sun enters Leo		
			28 JULY New Moon in Leo Jupiter stations retrograde in Aries			

JULY

SHELTER FROM
THE STORM

SHELTER FROM
THE STORM

Safe and sound inside its deep-sea secret locket, July's astrology asks us to sink down into hidden places – beckoning us home to the inner sanctuaries where we find our sense of belonging.

Shaded by the Moon-infused fourth sign, Cancer, it's a month made of covered coves and confidential diary entries, inviting us to engage with an internal process of incubation. Watching over all emergent acts of conception, July is a time to come back home to ourselves, tending to the private urges that live within us and conceiving of which embryonic imaginings we are getting ready to send down the birth canal.

A memory palace of moody made-for-television moments, July reminds us that every soapy feeling is part of our inner family system. Whether it's a previous reel from your own story, the root systems of your family of origin or a far more ancient inheritance, take July to check in with the past lives you're carrying in your antique treasure chest.

While we're sometimes sold a stereotype of cookie-baking Cancer energy filled with 'self-care' strategies that dunk us in bubble baths and cover us in rose petals, July wants us to take a more customized approach to attending to our inner caverns. This means engaging with a process of knowing what truly nourishes our souls, a line of inner enquiry that extends beyond surface security blankets and out into the wet and wild territory of intuitive self-awareness.

In the Tarot, Cancer is connected to The High Priestess, representing a silent sanctum that holds the seat of our deepest knowledge. Clutched close to our chests, this archetype asks us to embrace the whispers we can only hear in moments of solitary stillness. Notice when you feel overexposed to the light and long to glow in the dark of your own heart. Pay attention to how you rise to 'back' yourself when under attack. These moments are your tickets to protecting your own sensitive cycles.

Both private island and family-friendly beach bungalow, July indoctrinates us into the beauties of belonging, whether this means merging with others through shared midnight confessions or venturing into our depths with a solo skinny-dip that puts us back in touch with the safety net of our own skin. What arises when you think of being 'with' yourself? Loneliness? Fear? Ecstasy? And who are you really, when no one else seems to be watching? Whatever your orientation towards your inner swirl, July asks you to put the 'be' back in 'belonging'.

Let July be your permission slip to steep and to seep, submerging yourself in the hot tub of yearnings and embracing your liquid nature as you learn to move with the waters that move you. This month reminds us that to fully feel it is the fiercest act of all.

JULY DATES WITH DESTINY:
THE SLOW DANCE

This month, oceanic Cancer planets meet up with steady-on Taurus and Capricorn energy, and Aries' usual racing-car pace comes in for a pit stop as Chiron retrogrades. It's a month for relishing a slow, rhythmic unfolding, looking at our relationship to time and forgoing any hard-rock hustle for a more expansive R&B tempo. At its heart, linear time is a construct born of the belief that we must always be doing more and making better, ever moving towards a distant, more perfect vision of the future us. Yet when we look to nature, nothing is straight and all is swirling in a spiralling circuit of evolution in its own time. **July 2022 asks us to deconstruct our mental clocks, noticing where attachment to scheduled demands robs us of our sovereignty.** Start by noticing the 'order of operations' in your day: is an email check necessary before your first cup of tea? What deity is creating your deadlines? Your incarnation in this life is a brief, firefly blip – so make it last by making it your own.

Mercury enters Cancer
(enters Leo on 19th)

MISTY-COLOURED MEMORIES: It's a month to consider how we manufacture memories, as Mercury shifts into sepia-toned, scrapbook-happy Cancer. While it can feel utterly wild, and sometimes lonely, to consider that no two people ever remember the same event in the same way, it can also be liberating to release the controls around the way our stories get told. Start by considering a happening in your life that feels supercharged, one where you clutch the secret diary of its details to your chest like a moody teenager. What's beneath your need for this tale to be the end-all truth? And **what if you could use a time machine to take a peek at it from a different perspective?** Let this month be your DeLorean of destiny, reconsidering past details that in turn open up alternate future outcomes. When Mercury shifts into heart-on-sleeve Leo on the 19th, you'll be ready to harness any lingering sentimentalism – using past visions of greatness to prepare you for the party that lies ahead.

Mars enters Taurus

FEEL THE EARTH MOVE: Wait. Wait a little bit longer. What comes up for you in the spaces where it seems like 'nothing' is happening or you are attending a movement of the Earth? With the planet of mojo entering the Taurus boudoir of honeyed magnetics, this transit invites us to get comfy with taking actions that tangibly move us 'with' the natural turn of the Earth instead of against it. This doesn't mean we can't fight for what's right or must simply 'let it all be'. In contrast, **this is about rising to meet what's organically growing bigger in our lives**, like a surfer catching a massive wave, or a turbine harnessing the wild wind. Take a pause and listen in as you notice the landslide momentums in your life and *become* the energy of these elements, making like the weather to make it happen.

Full Moon in Capricorn

TIME AFTER TIME: An ancient and timeworn Moon, this well lived-in lunar event asks you to **pretend that you're the archaeologist of your life and start to excavate the interconnections between emotional artefacts.** Turn over the treasured pieces of yourself that have stood through all kinds of weather. Mine a historical event that seeded a currently bubbling realization, taking time to amplify time itself and notice where you're scrambling to get it done or you feel like time is running out. This Full Moon wraps you in the gorgeous arms of gravity, content to let the world turn on its axis and examine the layers of your life like the rings in a tree trunk.

Venus enters Cancer

PRIVATE EYES: Cancer is the seashell to Botticelli's Venus, and this transit asks us to consider when and how we choose to become 'naked' with life, **exploring our relationship to both our protective coverings and our moments of exposure.** Begin by examining your need for privacy. Maybe you're a deeply internal, nocturnal crab who craves hideaways. Or you might be more of a sea bird, who doesn't see the need for any covering at all, content to live your life on the sun-bleached shores. Whichever you are, take this transit to connect with where your heart longs to be right now and find your place in the sun or the shade.

Chiron stations retrograde in Aries
(until 23 December)

NO JACKET REQUIRED: A touchy-feely place, the planetoid Chiron is our skeleton key to the secret garden of sensitive humanness. And with its erratic orbit through the first sign of Aries lasting until 2026, we have plenty of time to make friends with this tender spot in our charts. Take this retrograde roll to **consider your birthright to simply 'be'.** While it may sound strange, many of us move through the world harbouring a subconscious belief that we have no right to be here in the first place. Stripped-down and singular, Aries energy reminds us that our existence is not an accident. In sticky moments of low self-esteem, remember that getting up, out of bed, and showing up is all that's required.

Sun enters Leo

EVERYTHING TO GIVE: The transition from Cancer's secret diary to Leo's heart-on-ruffled-sleeve approach is an invite to consider how we share ourselves with the world. **What would it take for you to give of yourself without elaborate asks in return** or carefully calibrated checks and balances? Not from a sense of martyred selflessness, but simply from the muscular act of heart opening, which is as natural as the Sun rising and a flower unfurling in its wake. Take this time to tap into your magnanimity – handing out your pink-ribboned heart packages with a trust that you'll never reach the bottom of this self-sustaining organ.

New Moon in Leo

FOLLOW THE SUN: Fashioned from a pocket-sized hot rock that's just beginning to glow, **this Moon invites us to instinctively reach for whatever is heating up in our lives.** Imagine that you're a kitten lounging on a patio as the day unfolds, only shifting its fluffy limbs to follow the sun. What's gone cold in your world, no longer providing any circulation or invigoration? Move away from it. What's getting marshmallow-toasty, filling your vital heart with radiance? Move towards it. No extra effort. No elaborate storylines. Just an attention to where there's warmth and an utterly uncomplicated response.

Jupiter stations retrograde in Aries
(until 23 November)

THE PERFECT FIT: As plus-sized palate-expander Jupiter slows down in free-to-be-me Aries, **this transit is an opportunity to look at how we insert and assert ourselves into the shape of life.** Begin by noticing anywhere you might be strong-arming yourself into a situation, project or even someone else's heart space. What if you could just expand side to side instead, becoming wider and then letting these projects and partnerships step inside *you* like a vast banqueting hall? Also consider any 'no's you're hearing right now, and how your ego might fire up when there's a perceived refusal. What if you could believe that another person's 'no' was actually a 'no' for your soul, too?

STAR PARTY: LUCKY SEVEN

From the seven wonders of the ancient world to the baby Buddha's first seven steps, and biblical tales of God resting on the seventh day, the number seven is imbued with multitudinous magical properties. Kabbalah, the Tarot and numerology all envision seven as a resting point where we gather strength for the next evolution spiral. In astrology, each of the seven weekdays is ruled by a separate planet. Explore the seventh month's call to follow your inner rhythms, as you check in with these planetary pulse points before overscheduling external commitments:

MONDAY: THE MOON – a day for tending the inner sanctum and nourishing emotional needs

TUESDAY: MARS – a day for bold initiations and life-force activations

WEDNESDAY: MERCURY – a day for integrating experiences and perusing the possibilities

THURSDAY: JUPITER – a day for roll-the-dice expansions and intuitive moves

FRIDAY: VENUS – a day for honeyed heart-opening and embodied enjoyment

SATURDAY: SATURN – a day for creating strong containers and drawing clear lines

SUNDAY: THE SUN – a day for standing out and celebrating your specialness

SIGN-BY-SIGN
GUIDE TO JULY

♋ CANCER

Happy birth time, little mermaid! The surf's up for you in July, as you dip into your deep end and find pleasure in flippered fantasy. While your sign sometimes gets positioned as the zodiac's mama bear – caretaking the clan with endless chicken soup for the soul – no matter your family status, July wants you to swaddle your own hopes and dreams with the same home-baked attention. What eggs are you incubating right now? Tend these precious promises of life with courage, consistency and your characteristic emotional nurturing – trusting that any seeds that are swelling inside you are worthy of guarding the same way you would a baby.

◆ With both Mercury and Venus meeting up in your sign, it's a perfect time to look at your fluctuations. Your oceanic energy both liberates life with each tidal shift and exerts powerful pulls on what you seek to keep for the long haul. Consider where you are right now in this cycle: is it a high-tide time where you're releasing and washing something onto shore, or a low-tide moment of pulling something back into your lair to have and to hold? Let this catch-and-release check-in help you find comfort within your cyclical cravings.

♌ LEO

Cuddling in the kitten basket wearing heart-shaped lockets, Leo and Cancer are here to guard and defend their right to love. Take July to consider the more inwardly facing properties of this juicy ardour – petting both your wounds and your wants with tender paws.

✦ As the calendar year cascades towards your sign's fiery solar entry onto the scene, and with Jupiter going retrograde in fellow Fire sign Aries, explore the way you 'build' excitement, finding enthusiasm in a steady amplification rather than a one-night-only blowout.

♍ VIRGO

Devotees of your inner altars, both Virgo and Cancer bow down to your own codes. Take July to add a little seawater to your sandcastles – forgoing some of your more granular efforts and micro-movements and letting the bigger emotional waves of give-and-take show you where to apply your adjustments.

✦ With Mars travelling through fellow Earth sign Taurus, July gives you extra room to move. Attend to any anxious moments where you spring into immediate action and explore what's pulsing beneath the surface when you commit to a pause.

J

♎ LIBRA

Born to turn down the extra bed in the guest room, Libra and Cancer are here to welcome in beloved others to better mirror their own self-understanding. Let July encourage you to allow ample time to look into your own eyes, too, and take back any parts that have been left behind.

+ With your ruler, Venus, in Cancer, facing off against Jupiter and Chiron in Aries, it is a profound moment for exploring any isolation fears. Where might you be buying into the belief that being completely yourself will leave you alone on a desert island?

♏ SCORPIO

The emotion ocean to your fixed ice and fiery steam, fellow Water sign Cancer is here to teach Scorpio that self-tending can be an act of self-celebration. Let July be a party for each of your most vividly felt feelings – as you become unafraid to explore both past and present highs and lows with the laid-back enjoyment of a slideshow of vacation photos.

+ With this month's Full Moon in survivalist Capricorn meeting up with evolutionary Pluto, you're asked to embrace the more glittery aspects of your grit. Make like an intrepid trailblazer and inspire others to get braver and bolder.

♐ SAGITTARIUS

The home and away of the zodiac, Cancer is the stable to Sagittarius' bareback ride. Down a dose of the crab's superpowers this month, as you book a return to the wondrous world that awaits you within – committing to the credo that internal adventures can be just as wild as the open road.

✦ With your ruler, Jupiter, stationing retrograde in Aries, there's magic medicine in stripping off the layers and finding elegance in the essentials. Consider where anything 'extra' feels more like a distraction than icing on the cake.

♑ CAPRICORN

Both Capricorn and Cancer are here to construct shelters made from equal parts strong foundation and supple feeling. Let Cancer's fluidity help you divine where you might be using your structuring principles to push away rather than stay with, exploring what you're keeping even from yourself when you hang a 'keep out' sign.

✦ With the Full Moon in your sign getting extra-special squeezes from evolutionary Pluto, Uranus and the North Node, scrap the need for externally sanctioned achievement and award yourself some accolades without looking for outside acceptance.

♒ AQUARIUS

Both restorative cleansers, Aquarius and Cancer replenish the rest of us with wisdom drawn from their own source waters. Let July be your invitation to explore who and what can care for you in the way that you care for the world – letting your most trusted spa confidantes turn on the taps and lay out the robes for a change.

✦ As your ruler, Uranus, touches in with the North Node in Taurus, check in with your relationship to relaxing and receiving. Where could you trade fired-up energy-wielding for a more open, inviting presence?

♓ PISCES

Sea sirens who set sail for imaginary islands, Pisces and Cancer share the power to channel intuitive hits that lead them to faraway lands. Sample some of Cancer's action-oriented Cardinal energy to fuel your dreams this month, taking pragmatic waking life steps to prop up your pillowed night-time visions.

✦ As Venus squares off with your ruler, Neptune, consider with compassion the parts of yourself you'd rather push away. While you don't have to fall head over heels for these sticky bits, you are invited to hear what they have to say.

♈ ARIES

The family home to your studio apartment, Cancer energy asks Aries to consider all the forces that commune to support and shape you. Let July be an opportunity to press pause on your permanent party for one and take an active interest in the beings and energies that want to lift and twirl you – trusting that your self-confident chants can also be sung in chorus.

✦ As the planet of existential meaning, Jupiter, stations retrograde in your sign, supercharge your spiritual search – opening yourself up to whatever you picture as 'greater' than you are and starting a deep and meaningful conversation with whichever goddess is calling to you.

♉ TAURUS

The daring downpour to your deep, fertile ground, Cancer's Cardinal Water is here to teach Taurus about your own capacity to acknowledge and absorb the full spectrum of feelings. Let July be a lesson in letting your longings just 'be' – allowing yourself to find the treasures in the wishing and wanting as much as the getting.

✦ With Mars, the North Node and Uranus all activated in your sign, notice any unconscious urges that don't necessarily serve your highest evolution. Rather than chastising yourself for choosing 'wrongly', just commit to calmly reaching in another direction.

♊ GEMINI

The hidden speakeasy to your sneakered street life, Cancer's whispered mysteries can challenge your urge for translation. Whether it's intel from a dream that you barely recall, or phrases overheard on a city bus that provoke an inexplicable feeling, use July to revel in everything that isn't immediately intelligible – applying your curiosity to life's unsolvable puzzles.

✦ With your ruler, Mercury, staging meet-and-greets with almost every planet on the block this month, don't worry if July feels a little zingy. Adopt any flightiness to flit about with glee, as you flirt with whoever and whatever crosses your rainbow-winged path.

STAR STYLE

COLOUR: Curl into molluscular and crepuscular shades like midnight blues and shimmering violets, the opalescent insides of conch shells, Impressionist water lilies, scarabs' sapphire backs and the darkness just before dawn.

FASHION: Find sanctuary in styles that draw from boudoir chic, ancient Greece or an artist's atelier in the south of France. Think underwear as outerwear, scalloped edges, bedroom eyes, fancy slippers, messy upswept hair, 1950s sweetheart necklines, lace smocks, low-slung trousers and slip-on mules. And whatever your look, treasure well-loved, storied pieces and swaddling-soft fabrics.

SCENT: July's aromas are salt-kissed and sentimental, conjuring coastal landscapes and safe interiors. Think sea-salt sprays, lotus flowers, tree resins and any olfactory remembrances that await you in the folds of timeworn sweaters, love letters, home spaces and beloved bodies.

FOOD FOR THE SOUL

Fortify your feelings with oceanic Mediterranean classic dishes, pocket-shaped provisions, fermented infusions and comfort foods. Think dumplings and samosas, clams, briny feta cheese and sardines, milk and honey, kimchi and pickled veggies.

CHART YOUR COURSE

July's energies ask us to travel down into the haunts and hideaways, relaxing into the locales where we best belong. Let your journeys be inspired by storied localities and sepia-toned sites of longing like Paris, Venice, ancient ruins, seaside towns and sacred grounds. Closer to home, find the courage to face the places that hold a potentially painful emotional charge for you, and seek solace in the homelands that always have your back.

ELEMENTAL EXCURSIONS

Cardinal Water-sign-ruled July is built for home-grown, nostalgic and nocturnal encounters. Think poring over yearbooks and scrapbooks, revisiting old record albums, DIY salt baths and body wraps, sharing private diary thoughts with a trusted circle, storybook romances and skinny-dipping.

PLANETARY PROMPTS

Use these magic words and journal
questions to moor you this month…

INCUBATION:

How can I handle my emotional ebbs and flows
and what's swirling within me right now?

PROTECTION:

What does tending to and caring for myself look like?

BELONGING:

Outside of traditional definitions, what
does home mean for me?

INHERITANCE:

What are the past 'origins' of present-day patterns and
which of these habits are no longer mine to carry?

BIRTHING:

Where am I ready to expand beyond my shell?

J

MONDAY	TUESDAY	WEDNESDAY	THURSDAY	FRIDAY	SATURDAY	SUNDAY
			4 AUGUST Mercury enters Virgo			
			11 AUGUST Venus enters Leo	**12 AUGUST** Full Moon in Aquarius		
					20 AUGUST Mars enters Gemini	
	23 AUGUST Sun enters Virgo	**24 AUGUST** Uranus stations retrograde in Taurus			**27 AUGUST** New Moon in Virgo	

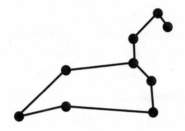

AUGUST

MAKE ROMANCE REAL

MAKE ROMANCE REAL

With a song in its heart and diamonds on the soles of its shoes, the astrology of August asks us to go in search of the gorgeous glow – putting our hands directly on life's warmth and presenting our presence like a pink-ribboned package that the world never knew it needed until right now.

Powered by the precious paw prints of the fifth sign, Leo, it's a sun-kissed month for touching and being touched by existence itself, as we exercise our right to see and be seen through the eyes of love. No matter which hemisphere you live in, imagine that August is your tropical honeymoon holiday, where the heat lasts all day and night and the air feels sweeter the closer it gets to your bare skin.

Following the tucked-in 'shell-ebrations' of Cancer-ruled July, August is our coming-out party. And while the month is packed with ripe fruits and fierce fun, it's also a chance to get real about our essence. August's Leonine energy urges us to make a peace pact with all parts of ourselves – looking our nature in the eye and celebrating each angle of our existence.

Leo's reputation for being the performer of the zodiac gets its power not from the applause of others but from an unshakable belief in the star-studded purpose that makes each of us utterly singular and wholly special. Our solid-gold nameplate necklace, August urges us to exercise our right to pen our personal signatures in neon lights. What flair can only you bring forwards by just being? And what would you do if August were your last month on Earth?

It's a month to believe that life can always be larger, an endless extravaganza of megawatt mythos. At its core, the concept of 'romance', also symbolized by Leo, extends beyond notions of partnership and into the realm of pure poetics – asking us to inject magic into the mundane. And when expressed in this manner, whether it's a sparkling sob fest, a sweat-drenched roller-skating session or simply the ability to notice the humorous hum of the teakettle, August is made for soundtracking your sidewalk struts and supersizing your hugs.

In visual representations of the Leo-ruled Strength card, we find a being dressed in cream befriending a beastly-looking lion. This unguarded stance activates August's simple and bold line of questioning: where have you steeled yourself against life's vivid, tender contours, believing that you'll only be hurt if you open your heart again? And where could you come closer to your own essence right now instead?

With nothing to lose, everything to give and just one life to live, August is a green light to leave your scent on the furniture and your lipstick on collars, pressing up against this one-and-only existence with irrepressible ardour. It asks you to ask yourself: *What do I love?* Whatever it is, say it louder.

A

AUGUST DATES WITH DESTINY:
CATCH + RELEASE

With the mercurial, Mutable energies of Gemini and Virgo encountering Fixed heavy-hitters Leo, Taurus and Aquarius, **August asks us to attend to both how we hold on to energy and how we ripen towards eventual release**. Fixed energy reaches a point of fullness that's so saturated it starts to spill over – opening us to the Mutable magic that then disperses it. Take August to place a beloved project, partnership or belief in a larger context, imagining that you're leaving it exposed in a wide-open field and letting the weather do its work around and upon it. Instead of worrying over the perception that you're giving something up, could you instead imagine that you're rendering it available for divine intervention?

Mercury enters Virgo
(enters Libra on 26th)

POCKET-SIZED PRAYERS: With Mercury entering its home turf of Virgo this month, it's a chance to polish our magnifying glasses and find the divine in every detail. While Virgo sometimes gets a rep for micromanagement, at its core this is less about filing cabinets and more about paying attention to the value in everything. Take this transit to sort out the difference between endless refinement that springs from a sense of 'never good enough' and a fine-tuned attention to the particulars that elevates them to artistry. **In your wild rush to get to work, what have you forgotten to notice?** Whether it's the smile lines on a lover's face or the still-tasty leftovers at the back of the fridge, take this transit to home in on human holiness.

Venus enters Leo

BEHOLD THE BEAUTY: As hedonistic Venus enters the sign that watches over both jungle cats and house kittens, the heat is turned up on our cravings to love and be loved. As your urges to reach out to others get buffed and polished, let this planetary shift bring you closer to the concept of 'beholding'. Far from needy asks, demands or calculated hunting of prey, **to behold another person, entity or idea is to simply hold them in love – free from judgement, assessment or any urge to adjust.** Take this time to consider what in your life inspires amorous awe and wonderment.

Full Moon in Aquarius

THE GRAND PLAN: The Leo–Aquarius polarity invites us onto the fully lit dance floor – and lets our particularity collide with other partygoers grooving in tune to a universal heartbeat. This Full Moon wants you to **get eccentrically existential and consider that you are a conduit for a much larger purpose.** Are there moments when you feel wildly uncomfortable or out of your depth, when you can sense that you're here to bring something forward or to move energy that's not about the 'little' you at all? Whether it's a healing of your ancestral lineage or a leadership role in this lifetime, let this lunar event inspire one step for your own specialness and a giant leap for humankind.

Mars enters Gemini

A PIÑATA: With go-getter Mars in grab-bag Gemini, surprise sources of fuel await us around every corner. Take this planetary passage to explore where you get 'stuck' going to the same old source for inspo or activation. Whenever you notice that you're beginning a project in rote fashion or are entrenched in a relationship dynamic of pre-scripted roles, **let a little divine distraction direct you towards alternative solutions.** Take a brisk walk around the block. Blast an unfamiliar tune. Awaken your senses with some spice. Reaching with eyes closed into the variety pack of life uncovers new power party moves.

Sun enters Virgo

SIGNATURE SCENTS: The Sun's shift from Leo's beach party to Virgo's witchy woods invites us to make good on the promise of our essence – taking our new-found knowledge about the stuff we're made of and crafting it into an intricate, integral inner code. Like a perfumer or sommelier picking out individual notes in a blend, let this cosmic changeover be your opportunity to comb through your own contents. **What precious parts have you known to be true for all time? And how does each of these aspects of yourself 'serve' you?** Consider the magic medicine in every piece of your personhood – divining precisely which of your superpowers to apply to a given situation.

A

Uranus stations retrograde in Taurus
(until 22 January 2023)

FLOWER FOOD: Halfway through a seven-year cycle in Taurus, Uranus in this pleasure-ready sign has asked us all to rethink our sources of sustenance and to consider what truly feeds our souls. Now, with the change-making planet rolling retrograde, we're invited to let our physical vessels fully take the lead. Notice where you might have become a 'talking head' – pushing through work when it's time for a snack, or going against a gut instinct in the name of being polite. **What lies beneath the belief that your body doesn't deserve what it wants?** Taurus teaches us that we are made from the same matter as all Earth's flora and fauna. So make like a fancy rosebush and give your root systems exactly the flower food they need.

New Moon in Virgo

EVERYDAY ALCHEMY: While you may or may not identify with the word 'witch', we all contain our own custom cauldrons where we mix our energy with earthly matter – alchemizing the stuff of life into our own custom blends. Take this New Moon to look at the everyday materials around you and the inner magic you can apply to combine, refine and draw new manifestations to the surface. Nothing is too mundane to include in this process; know that your 'soul work' might take the form of anything from accounting to child-rearing to opera singing. **Let this cosmic event remind you of your power to change the world through careful attention and curation** of its constituent parts.

A

STAR PARTY:
THE LION'S GATE PORTAL (8 AUGUST)

On the 8th, we pass through the supercharged Lion's
Gate Portal. Marked by the astral alignment of the
Earth and the star Sirius, which becomes visible in the
eastern sky around the 8th, and a meet-up between
the Orion constellation and Egypt's Pyramids of Giza,
the Lion's Gate has been a spiritual power point for
thousands of years. Magnified by the magic of the
number eight, it's a cosmic happening that ignites
our creative force on every level. Let this portal be
your chance to boldly declare your most heart-
centric intentions, as you commit to living wholly
and solely from the seat of your most vivid self.

SIGN-BY-SIGN
GUIDE TO AUGUST

♌ LEO

Happy birth month, little love cat! August is your time to purr for what's most precious, as you let this month be your chance to fall in love again with life itself. While this may sound abstract, consider the mutual admiration that naturally develops when you look upon the world with amorous eyes; like a tender plant smooched by the big old Sun, wherever you choose to point your gaze is warmed by your attention alone. Leo's Fixed heat is the hearth of the zodiac, here to welcome even the hardest of hearts in from the cold. Invite the world to soften towards you this month, melting the ice of any guarded fears and reaching out to pet the planet.

✦ With Venus in your sign this month meeting an entire party of planets, it's a magic moment for considering all of the shapes and shades of love. While we sometimes get hung up on strict definitions of duration, commitment, healthy vs unhealthy and successful matches vs 'failed' tries, could you be available for the full rainbow of romance this August? From the briefest of encounters to making a lifelong commitment, trust that every communion with another human has a full purpose and a holy completeness.

♍ VIRGO

Two essential oils of originality, both Virgo and Leo share a sense of uniqueness that springs from a celebration of their specificity. Let August be a chance to drop any analytics in favour of an *al dente* pasta approach – joyously sharing parts of yourself with the world spontaneously and seeing what sticks to the wall.

+ A 'trine' aspect describes when planets come together to form a diamond ring of support. With Mercury in your sign trining the North Node, Uranus and Pluto, this month is an opportunity to marry yourself to new mantras – stopping any mental spin-outs dead in their tracks.

♎ LIBRA

With a penchant for creating serene sculptures out of rock, both Libra and Leo revel in life's ideals. Take a page out of Leo's party planner about the art of acceptance – celebrating the naturally beautiful elements of life that are allowed to simply come as they are.

+ With Mars in fellow Air sign Gemini this month, swap the straight lines for a little zigzag action – forgoing a rigid focus on getting from A to B and enjoying what wildflowers can be found when you see off-road detours as curious opportunities.

A

♏ SCORPIO

Symbolized by the lion and the scorpion respectively, Leo and Scorpio are the only two unabashed carnivores of the zodiac. Make meaty magic this month by letting any fears that something is 'too much' fade into the background, embracing your status as a jungle creature who's here to hunt down whatever snacks take your fancy.

✦ The 'opposition' aspect asks us to partner with the two planets in a face-off, remaining conscious of which side we might push away. As Venus opposes your ruler, Pluto, it's a month to let what you supposedly loathe remind you of your passionate life force, using strong aversions as unexpected rocket fuel.

♐ SAGITTARIUS

Sagittarius and Leo are ruled by Jupiter and the Sun respectively, which both ask us to expand our self-confidence and self-trust. Use August to remember your right to choose yourself without its having to serve a higher cause, finding faith that some healthy self-centredness will naturally align you with what the world needs now.

✦ With Mars heading into your opposite sign of Gemini, embrace adaptive action – notice where you're gripping tightly to one way of doing things and swap force for flexible trials and outcomes.

♑ CAPRICORN

The governess of Leo's unruly children, Capricorn is here to wrangle exuberant leonine excesses back into line. Yet both signs share a taste for luxury that requires regal treatment and diamond-cut finery. Activate this appetite for high-end living in August, licking your chops and exercising your right to demand excellence on every occasion.

+ The 'quincunx' aspect – when signs of both contrasting elements and modalities come together – invites self-discovery through compassionate curiosity. With Gemini and Leo energies in quincunx to your sign this month, learn about yourself through osmosis – brushing shoulders with what seems unlike you instead of using it as evidence of your deficiencies.

♒ AQUARIUS

Dance partners who lift one another towards the highest creative potential, Leo strikes its signature moves while Aquarius stages the spectacle to best inspire the crowd. Let August remind you of the heartbeat behind the scenery, as you infuse your cool and calm director status with the right to claim passionate authorship of the performance.

✦ This month's Full Moon in your sign wants you to get a little bit 'loony' – forgoing any complicated explanations and letting the reasons behind your choices and cravings remain delightfully mysterious, even to you.

✵ PISCES

Connected by a shared appreciation for Hollywood glamour, both Leo and Pisces see the star-studded quality in even the most so-so stuff of life. Let this month remind you to use this sense of poetry to bring you closer to what you love – getting healthily attached without having to seek an escape hatch from heightened emotion.

✦ As your honorary ruling planetoid, Chiron, touches in with Venus this month, explore any haunted places that seem to be keeping you from fully 'hoping' – transforming wishful thinking into a self-affirming act that challenges any deprivation fears.

♈ ARIES

Both Aries and Leo are emboldened Fire babes here to gift their glow to a world in need of thawing. Let August be your chance to stabilize some of your spark – settling down in front of the hearth and letting passions build before they pop. Remember that your heart is a muscle, so make sure any power moves are infused with pure love.

✦ With your ruler, Mars, meeting up with both the North Node and Uranus this month, it's a chance to get just a little bit 'possessed'. Let yourself follow the force of full-bodied pulls to certain actions, even if they feel beyond your conscious control.

♉ TAURUS

Here to embrace the plush stuffed animals of life, Taurus and Leo clutch their passions to their chests – seeking creature comforts and Fixed-sign fascinations that are firmly fastened down. This month, borrow some of Leo's eternal flame and remind yourself that any pledges of loyalty are as much about finding pleasure in your own integrity as they are about 'possessing' something or someone outside of yourself.

✦ Your ruler, Venus, makes a flurry of 'aspects' this month, which is astro code for a planet brushing up against and learning from its neighbours. Take this time to play dress-up with what pleases you – try all kinds of passion projects on for size.

♊ GEMINI

A block party of bold moves and curious chips and dips, Gemini and Leo are both here to get into the groove and stay open-minded, no matter the hard knocks. Let August be an invitation to sample some

A

of Leo's sense of courageous commitment, affixing some heart-shaped stickers to life and claiming bragging rights to your beloveds.

✦ With Mars powering up for its entry into your sign later in the month, cut the analysis and just come out with it, even if it seems half-cocked – trusting that your plans don't need to feel fully ready to get green-lit in the eyes of goddess.

♋ CANCER

'Semi-sextile' or 'cusp' signs that sit side by side and are asked to cheer each other on, Cancer incubates an inner vision while Leo grabs it and sends it off into the world. Embrace some of this 'exposure' in August, stepping out from the shade and into the self-expressive sunlight without shying away from being truly seen.

✦ With this month's Moon cycle energies occurring in the signs of Aquarius and Virgo, it's time to embrace your eccentricities – find wonder in your weirdness, even when it seems to set you apart from the safety of the pack.

STAR STYLE

COLOUR: Celebrate your specialness with fully saturated jewel tones, glowing, sun-kissed shades, playground primaries and rainbow sherbets. Think peachy pinks, red-hot cherries, creamy lemon sorbets, mouth-watering magentas and scorching corals.

FASHION: Imagine a Vegas showgirl vacationing in the tropics, with fluff, bronzer, rainbow leopard print, gaudy turquoise eye shadow, candy necklaces, gold lamé, oversized ruby baubles and glossy lips. And no matter your penchant for performance, embrace a look that's utterly and wholly you by picking a piece of personal 'flair' to add to your ensemble and magnifying your mane – whether it's voluminous pink locks or a bald head polished to a high shine.

SCENT: August's aromas are infused with playful perfumes and over-the-top, juicy explosions. Think bubblegum, citrus gourmand scents, inexpensive body sprays as well as designer perfumes, suntan oil and the aroma left in your wake as you walk through the world.

A

FOOD FOR THE SOUL

Celebrate sun-baked succulence and seamless self-expression with ripe, tender tomatoes, citrus squeezes, creamsicles, Caprese salad, open-faced sandwiches and tropical infusions like coconut soda, mango salsa, pineapple pizza and plantains.

CHART YOUR COURSE

August's energies ask us to come at life with hands out and hearts bared – closing the 'space' between ourselves and what surrounds us. Travel to lands where the temperature remains toastily steady and an expressive ethos runs the show. Think equatorial escapes, the palatial kitsch of Las Vegas, Rome's delectable drama and Miami's heat. Closer to home, develop your personal map to the stars by engaging in some 'see and be seen' action at your most treasured spots, and leave little traces as you go – whether it's your number on a napkin or your initials carved in a tree.

ELEMENTAL EXCURSIONS

Fixed Fire-sign-ruled August is ripe for glamorous guilelessness and sensational simplicity. Think dressed-up bedroom dance parties, heart-on-sleeve pop anthems, shopping mall makeovers, beachfront carnivals, roller-skating, stuffed-animal pile-ups, losing the 'guilt' from any and all pleasures, and anything that offers earnest immersion in the present moment.

PLANETARY PROMPTS

Use these magic words and journal
questions to moor you this month…

EXPOSURE:

How does it feel to be 'seen' and where
might I show more of myself?

ROMANCE:

What connects me to a larger-than-
life sense of sparkle and flair?

DISARMAMENT:

Where can I go 'heart-first' and share
my tenderness more freely?

PRESENCE:

What is asking for me to simply
'behold' it without analysis?

SELF-EXPRESSION:

What is my signature brand of specialness
and what can only I gift to the world?

A

MONDAY	TUESDAY	WEDNESDAY	THURSDAY	FRIDAY	SATURDAY	SUNDAY
5 SEPTEMBER Venus enters Virgo					**10 SEPTEMBER** Full Moon in Pisces Mercury stations retrograde in Libra	
				16 SEPTEMBER Sun in Virgo opposite Neptune in Pisces		
				23 SEPTEMBER Sun enters Libra		**25 SEPTEMBER** New Moon in Libra

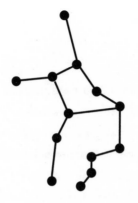

SEPTEMBER

WORK YOUR MAGIC

WORK YOUR MAGIC

A custom cologne crafted from the wild woods within, the astrology of September asks us to kneel at our inner altars – anointing ourselves in the signature scents of self-understanding so that we can bring our unique mystique to the world.

Wed to the witchery of the sixth sign of Virgo, this month is for letting our constituent parts come into clarity, as we take an inventory of our assets and mine our own mineral make-up for magic. After the exuberant self-expression of August and its Leo energies, September is our back-to-school cosmic chemistry class – an invitation to calibrate the bespoke beakers bubbling with the properties that compose our holistic whole.

Before the sign's symbol of a virgin was co-opted by the patriarchy, the figure representing Virgo was simply an unmarried woman who chose to live by her own laws and to never, ever give it away for free. To embrace the sign's motto, 'I serve', we must first and foremost serve with fierce fealty at the altar of self. As the sign that arrives just before the zodiac's midway point, Virgo marks the last moment we have solely to ourselves before we step into the wider collaborative communion of the final six signs.

Ruled by The Hermit card in the Tarot, Virgo asks us to pay

a visit to a self-curated cabin in the woods, using our precious time to take stock as we digest and integrate our experiences and appraise and refine our resources. A master class in meteorology, September's Virgoan vineyard teaches us to read the weather and embrace the *terroir* of our lives, dressing for the seasonal shift and waiting for precisely the right moment to step outside. Take this month to align yourself with the perfectly imperfect order of nature itself – curating your life organically, without editorializing or critiquing, as you simply sieve the best and the brightest from each plant, animal and mineral in your garden.

As for its opposite sign of Pisces, and its fellow Mercury-ruled nervous system-channeller, Gemini, Virgo's Mutable energy serves as a spiritual medium. The month beckons us to bolster a deep trust in our own physicality so that we can 'take the shape', letting life come through us and unto us as we apprentice ourselves to our very existence. A vestal vessel that humbles us to the hum of each divine detail, Virgo's humility is far from powerless – born instead from the belief that knowing exactly what we're made of lets us share our gifts most authentically.

Take September to bow down to your nature. To keep your own time. To discern your personal pattern as though you are reading the back of a leaf or the sound of the wind. So steeped in your seasonal self-consideration that you can submit to the wild weather that wants to move through you – and to the wild notion that you, too, are a part of every living thing.

S

SEPTEMBER DATES WITH DESTINY:
ASTRO ACCOUNTABILITY

With all outer planets (Jupiter, Saturn, Uranus, Neptune and Pluto) now rolling retrograde, Mercury slowing down to join the mix and the equinox's energy amplifying the theme of alignment, **September is an opportunity to take stock of where we are and how we think we got here.** Are you defining your circumstances against a rubric of external values, believing that where you find yourself at this stage of your life is largely down to something or someone outside of yourself? Or do you believe that every last thing is your 'fault' and yours alone? Take this month to look at who and what you think is 'responsible' for the circumstances of your life, finding a balance between shouldering the burdens of the world and placing the blame.

Venus enters Virgo
(enters Libra on 29th)

LOVE IS ALSO A VERB: As the planet of amorous exchange enters the sign of daily devotion, it's time to commit to the credo that all shades of love require care. Whether it's romance, friendship or a creative project, there are no longevity givens in love; **each day is a new opportunity to show your commitment to what you adore.** Whether it's a home-cooked meal for a beloved or a constitutional walk to show your body how much you care, turn your ardour into action imbued with clear intention. When Venus enters its home turf of Libra on the 29th, it'll be time to assess how to equilibrate these amorous actions – exploring how your displays of love are received and which are most worthy of your continued efforts.

Full Moon in Pisces

GONE BUT NOT FORGOTTEN: Full Moons signal powerful completions and celebratory harvests. In the last of the 12 zodiac signs, this one can feel like the be-all and end-all of a part of our lives that has reached its highest capacity. And while there might be grief involved in letting go, take this Moon to remember that **whatever is ending can also just fade, becoming part of the woodwork and**

your inner workings. Like a person who passes away but lives on through memories and shared gestures, this lunar event wants you to know that even amid extreme 'absence', nothing is ever truly gone.

Mercury stations retrograde in Libra
(re-enters Virgo on 23rd; stations direct on 2 October)

BALANCING ACTS: Mercury's slowdown in Libra is an opportunity to consider what equilibrium looks like for us. **How we experience harmony depends on our capacity to decide how to apportion our energy**, forgoing any perfection-driven checks for the fluidity of continual calibration. Take this retrograde cycle to adjust the knobs in whatever direction is calling your attention, remembering that balance might mean sending extra energy in a particular direction while leaving other areas temporarily left to their own devices.

Sun in Virgo opposite Neptune in Pisces

BECOME INVISIBLE: Virgo and Pisces energies invite us to celebrate our status as dazzling specks in the Universe – Virgo's microscope magnifies each tiny star and Pisces bathes itself in the sky's entirety. Take this transit to practise the art of 'invisibility'. **Imagine that you could become one with your environment and not have to**

try so hard to be constantly seen. Let this feel relaxed rather than like an act of self-repression: release yourself from any need to be constantly 'on' and surrender into the scenes that surround you.

Sun enters Libra

NATURAL SELECTION: The Sun's transition from Virgo's organic alignments into Libra's aesthetic ideals is a carefully choreographed ballet. An opportunity to choose your music and move with grace and vision, it reminds you that you are the arbiter of your experience. **You know your tastes. And you know what doesn't serve your system.** Pair yourself with what supports your natural make-up – choosing what's most right for you, right now.

New Moon in Libra

LIFE ON THE OTHER SIDE: Libra energy invites us to enjoy a dance with life that alternates between coming close and pushing back. Take this New Moon to consider what projects, people and parts of yourself you're drawing near to and which you're fighting off. **Where you've adopted a 'hard no' or a 'hell, yes', pause and consider the reason.** That way, you'll ensure that your logic is completely sound on a soul level.

S

STAR PARTY:
EQUINOX (23 SEPTEMBER)

At our first equinox in March, the Sun's ingress into
fiery Aries took the lead. And now we're cooling down
on the other side as the Sun enters Libra territory.
Amplified by the Libra-ruled Justice card in the Tarot,
it's a cosmic happening that asks us to explore our
relationship to the principles of fate and free will. Take
this equinox (called the autumn equinox in the northern
hemisphere and the spring equinox in the southern
hemisphere) to forgo the extremes and choose your
destiny instead, letting an alignment with what's
actually right for you fuel a sense of larger rightness,
as you summon the courage to do what you 'must'.

SIGN-BY-SIGN
GUIDE TO SEPTEMBER

♍ VIRGO

Happy birth month, inner witch! September is your moment to venerate your internal code, developing a deeply felt sense of exactly what you are and are not available to accommodate any longer. But rather than a ferociously geometric act of boundary-setting, can you instead let this feel like a stripping down in order to let yourself be better 'found' by life? Imagine that a new project, partnership or way of being is already on its way to you. How might you make space at your table, sending up a 'flare' for this newness to know you're ready and willing? Clear out the cobwebs of expired energies and keep your candle lit for what's coming.

+ With pleasure palace Venus also joining up with your sign this month, September is a time to consider how you honour your own maturation process. When's the last time you took a day, or even an hour, to make a toast to an emotional win? While we're accustomed to celebrating the more tangible touchstones, like weddings, births and career pinnacles, we tend to forget the lost art of marking our subtler self-development shifts. Let this month be your call to lay out the party plates for a personal turning point.

♎ LIBRA

Virgo and Libra are figures in the sculpture garden of the cosmos, with Libra building on Virgo's natural selection process to further elevate what rises to the surface. Take September to swap any too rigidly held standards for Virgo's more organic order, as you embrace the beautiful 'mess' that can sort itself out without your having to manage it.

✦ As the year's final Mercury retro rolls through your sign, let yourself see what's here without needing to take immediate action, using your consummate capacity for clarity to watch the dust settle before leaping to wipe the surfaces down.

♏ SCORPIO

The zodiac's celestial surgeons, both Virgo and Scorpio know how to slice through the extraneous and get straight to the beating heart of the matter. This month, let Virgo's carefully coiled power remind you that you can choose exactly which 'organs' need to be excised – homing in on what counts and not wasting one drop of your superpowers.

✦ With your honorary ruler, lusty lunar point Lilith, communing with the North Node and Chiron this month, consider the

S

benefits of keeping your beasts at bay, catching yourself before you blow your lid to assess whether your target is truly worth the energy.

♐ SAGITTARIUS

Virgo and Sagittarius are each on a celestial scavenger hunt, in search of meaning and magic in every crack and fissure. Use September to recover the divine detective within, as you fine-tune your ability to read the signs and let even the seemingly oppressive stuff of the everyday world be a potential clue about your next move.

✦ As Mercury faces off against your ruler, Jupiter, it's a perfect time to consider your energetic metabolism. Rather than leaping into largesse, start by sampling tiny tastes of a new way of being as you build up to the whole cake.

♑ CAPRICORN

Two Earth babes built for the long haul, Capricorn weatherizes against the elements, while Virgo reads the meteorology report. Remember that you don't always have to anticipate and protect against potential storms, as you loosen some of the sealant on your ski lodge to let in more of life's glorious snowfall.

✦ As the Sun finds support from evolutionary Pluto in your sign this month, consider where you might celebrate the process of self-development – remembering that soul growth doesn't always have to be soul-shakingly brutal.

♒ AQUARIUS

Both gifted seers who can spot what's ready to shift from miles away, Virgo and Aquarius are the zodiac's interstellar marker pens, underlining their strategies across life's whiteboards. Borrow some of Virgo's appreciation for the fine lines this month as you temper a little bit of your urge to immediately break out of the box with some curiosity about the liberating potential of limits.

✦ With your ruler, Uranus, meeting up with the lunar point Lilith this month, consider the adage that all change comes from the inside. Forgo forced efforts at external fixing for some time spent sitting with the more ineffable shifts within.

♓ PISCES

Arguably the most sensitive souls in the zodiac, Pisces and Virgo are the primed antennae who absorb the environment surrounding them. This month, borrow some of Virgo's earthier essence and dive deep into the details, rather than floating above the surface.

S

✦ As both the Sun and Venus face off against your ruler, Neptune, explore where you might be sacrificing yourself at the altar of being too 'nice'. Consider that sharing your true feelings with others can be the greatest love of all.

♈ ARIES

Two self-calibrated cosmic kiddies, Aries and Virgo are fiercely focused and divinely driven. Let September be your ticket to swap any 'all or nothing' finish lines for some of Virgo's adaptable peripheral vision, remembering that any course corrections are courageous co-creative acts, rather than evidence of finite failure.

✦ With this month's equinox marking the six-month point since your birthday season, take September to digest the ride you've been on this year – trusting that the work right now is invisibly occurring beneath the surface without needing to be known.

♉ TAURUS

From the careful process of vineyard cultivation to a Taurine feast on the grapes, Virgo is here to teach Taurus about the pleasures of attending to life's complexities. Let September be your invitation to step into it subtly – swapping one-note notions of how things are for a more intricate examination of the evidence.

✦ With the North Node in your sign gaining support from lunar point Lilith this month, shine a light on habitual grooves, noticing where you might temporarily sacrifice some immediate comfort for a longer-term blanket of support.

♊ GEMINI

Co-ruled by metabolic Mercury, both Virgo and Gemini are complex channellers who catch and distribute the ineffable matter that swirls through the air. Take September to remind yourself that you are the gatekeeper of your open-and-shut valve, choosing which energy makes it through your selective sieve and onto your supper plate.

✦ With Mercury's final retrograde roll in your element of airy unfolding, wield your voice with the maturity of a well-seasoned opera singer – trusting in intel gleaned through experience and committing to your personal perspective without having to toe the party line.

♋ CANCER

Both fertile forces who blossom from the inside out, Virgo and Cancer are called to carefully care for their own interiors. Embrace some of Virgo's more pragmatic self-care this month, as you attend to the moments when you expect another person to 'hold' your big feelings, and make sure you've hugged them yourself first and foremost.

✦ With this month's Pisces and Libra Moons powered by dream-weaver Neptune and pleasure-seeker Venus, take time to commune with the good, the true and the beautiful, sourcing sweetness wherever it may be found.

♌ LEO

Bound by a heightened awareness of their sparkly specialness, both Virgo and Leo are asked to apply the warmth of their life force with vigour and verve. This month, borrow from Virgo's sense of discernment to temper your sometimes voraciously self-depleting generosity, choosing exactly who and what is deserving of your presence.

✦ With Virgo and Libra planets emphasizing the art of alignment and calibration, take time to consider how you could 'hold' some of your heat – trusting that putting yourself on a simmer can be an act of self-love rather than self-repression.

STAR STYLE

COLOUR: Embrace nature's palette and the nuance of film noir with soft metallics: rose gold, the gold of shifting sands, the silver of tumbled stones and the copper of wheatfields; along with cameo creams and salmon pinks.

FASHION: Conjure up a 1930s starlet communing with a Santa Fe naturalist in Elizabethan England. Think kaftans, intricate art deco jewellery, copper lockets, high ruffled necks, gilded patterning, buttons on sleeves, lace-up sandals, suede booties and broad-brimmed hats. And whatever your self-chosen silhouette, pledge allegiance to your private places with the inward-facing artistry of a tiny hidden tattoo, nail polish on your toes even though they're tucked into socks, or a for-your-eyes-only piece of lingerie.

SCENT: September's aromas are medicinally magical and harvested from the earth's natural healers. Think camphor, citronella, holy basil, tea tree, bergamot, *herbes de Provence* and lavender pillows.

S

FOOD FOR THE SOUL

Sample trusted, integral flavours, herbaceous blends and careful concoctions like rosemary-infused fresh bread, tisanes, hot cobbler with seasonal fruits, subtly spiced soups, pestos, harvest grains, dried apricots, frisee and strained labneh.

CHART YOUR COURSE

September's energies invite us to align our internal and external worlds, paying homage to both our personal weather patterns and the earthly elements that surround us. Travel to landscapes where humans honour holistic living and refined ritual. Think permaculture farms, health spas, bed and breakfasts, vineyards, the south of France, the eco-conscious city of Portland in Oregon and the simply sublime shrines of Kyoto, Japan. Closer to home, forge an alliance with the intricacies of your environment by engaging in seasonally specific activities and visiting hyper-local haunts with a strong sense of place.

ELEMENTAL EXCURSIONS

Mutable Earth-sign-ruled September is fit for everyday alchemy, considered corporeality and self-governed sensuality. Think food and beverage pairings, ritual baths, herb gardening, Ayurveda, perfume making, unusual miniatures, lingerie shopping, solitary sauntering, closet cleaning, farmers' markets and making something beautiful out of whatever's close at hand.

PLANETARY PROMPTS

Use these magic words and journal
questions to moor you this month...

INTEGRITY:

What is my 'essence' and which
fundamental qualities am I made of?

ALCHEMY:

Which metaphorical season of life do I find myself
in, and how can I respond to the current weather?

RITUAL:

How can I support my inner rhythms through daily acts?

DEVOTION:

What's asking for my attention, and how
can I show up to fully serve this?

CRAFT:

What am I learning to master in this lifetime,
and how can I let myself be 'in process'?

S

MONDAY	TUESDAY	WEDNESDAY	THURSDAY	FRIDAY	SATURDAY	SUNDAY
						2 OCTOBER Mercury stations direct in Virgo
					8 OCTOBER Pluto stations direct in Capricorn	**9 OCTOBER** Full Moon in Aries
						23 OCTOBER Sun and Venus enter Scorpio Saturn stations direct in Aquarius
	25 OCTOBER New Moon in Scorpio (partial solar eclipse)					**30 OCTOBER** Mars stations retrograde in Gemini

OCTOBER

EVERYTHING IS
ILLUMINATED

EVERYTHING IS
ILLUMINATED

A poised *pas de deux* with our polarity points, October's astrology asks us to engage in the art of aligned assessment – exploring both what we think we 'are' and 'are not'. It brings an opportunity to reconcile our dualities so we can reach out to one another across any perceived divides, travelling arm-in-arm towards our highest hopes and elevating our shared existence.

Shaped by the curatorial clarity of the seventh sign, Libra, it's a month made for making moves beyond the 'small' self – considering the confluences, compromises and crossroads that take us from personal drive to full participation. October asks us to use any new-found self-knowledge to fuel our actions in the wider world – letting what's right for us synchronize and synergize with the reality that surrounds us.

Sprung completely intact from the head of Zeus in the guise of wisdom warrior Athena, Libra performs smooth slices with a steady arm – asking us to lock eyes with all that rests outside our orbit, as we let life meet us on its own terms. October's energy suggests we allow things to be exactly as they are before we slip on our rose-coloured spectacles.

Ruled by the Justice card in the Tarot, Libra season is when we learn to regard what's real in order to refine it. Imbued with the number 11, this archetype conjures images of balance beams and Olympic luges – a chance to straighten up and fly right. But October also wants us to let 'balance' be a dynamic dance of reflection and course-correction, as we divine precisely what's asking for more or less of our attention in every moment.

What's presenting itself on your doorstep, pure and simple, regardless of how you might feel about it? And which pieces of your world do you feel like you can't – or won't – deal with? That aren't for you or about you? Libra energy asks us to catch our lives in a serenely executed ice-skating lift, spinning matter with mature calculation and equal parts grit and grace.

Take a moment to recall times in your life when you experienced a naturally synchronized alignment between what you knew to be true for you and a way that you were being asked to show up in the world. Or a time when you fiercely called it quits on a pattern because it just no longer served. Far from a guilty 'no' that pushes us away from 'bad' habits and punishes our deviations, October's energy asks us to simply summon the courage to do what we already know we must.

A serenity prayer to the cosmos, it's a month for harnessing the wisdom to know the difference between what we can and cannot change. And to find the power to pave a path towards what could be – dreaming this dream together by first daring to stand face to face.

O

OCTOBER DATES WITH
DESTINY: SOUL SURVIVORS

With steamy Aries and Scorpio Moons, power-pusher Pluto stationing direct and an action-packed Mars retrograde, the energies of October are full-on and fierce. Amid all of this evolutionary intensity, **we're asked to dig deep beneath our primal patterning to see what really runs the show – bringing greater consciousness to our kneejerk survival mechanisms.** Start by noticing when you have a gargantuan reaction to something seemingly innocuous: a flood of tears provoked by a small comment; an unquenchable hunger in the face of an external limit. These primal pulse points are the keys to transforming reactivity into more consciously channelled force. Boldly breathe into anything that provokes a strong 'charge' and then choose exactly what fires you'd like it to ignite.

Mercury stations direct in Virgo
(re-enters Libra on 10th; enters Scorpio on 29th)

THE WORK IS THE WORK: With Mercury now rolling upright until the end of the year, October is a chance to approach our own self-development with unsanctimonious simplicity. The trio of Virgo, Libra and Scorpio indoctrinates us into a cycle of self-examination, reckoning, integration and clearing, where **healing is always close and present – each aspect of our lives an opportunity to engage in necessary evolution**. Take this time to assess the growth opportunities that exist without having to journey to fancy mountaintops, considering that your emotional 'work' can be found more proximately. Whatever feels like your 'same old' spin cycle is precisely what you're meant to be mastering, and it naturally arises in even the most mundane of moments. Let feelings that come up while chopping the veggies, phoning the plumber or debating with loved ones be your gateways towards enlightenment.

8

Pluto stations direct in Capricorn

OVER + DONE: Evolutionary excavator Pluto's retrograde roll through Capricorn, which began at the end of April, asked us to let it come 'undone', as we learned to release our futile fight to keep it all 'together'. And now, with this big old beastie moving forward, it's a tough-love time for just getting on with it all – armed with info about the old order that has already been overturned. This is not to say that we have to repress our tender emotions or not tend to our softer spaces. But it is a call to **consider our finite time on planet Earth and what we just can't engage with anymore.** Chances are, you know exactly what this means. What landslides in your life have already been bringing down patterns primed for purging? And how can you agree to participate in this overthrow? There are things you cannot unsee. Knowledge you now have that you can't unknow. Face up to the facts and call a stop on what's no longer fit.

Full Moon in Aries

THE IMPACT REPORT: Like a construction project impact report or an earthquake Richter scale, the Aries Full Moon wants you to consider the real-time effects of various parts of your world. **Start by engaging in a little emotional cost-benefit life analysis**. How much does a particular behaviour, relationship or activity take away from your energetic force, and how much does it give back? How do these components echo out, creating ripples in other areas of your life? Stay sweet with yourself as you explore this assessment process, remembering that there's no reason to regret or self-punish. Instead, treat this time as a celebration of your own self-consideration and authorial intent, as you identify what takes too much out of your cosmic bank to justify its continued existence, and exercise your right to select what supports your longevity.

Sun and Venus enter Scorpio

THE GOOD, THE BAD AND THE HUMAN: The transition between Libra and Scorpio seasons takes us on a journey to the heart of our humanness – representing a rich reckoning with all that's contained within us and around us, which paves the path towards **lasting intimacy born from letting ourselves and others be exactly as we are.** Originally considered as one sign that shared the same constellation – with Libra forming the Scorpion's sharp claws – this transition represents an opportunity to assess where we categorize parts of our being, our experience and the people we encounter as either good or bad. While all humans have an innate desire to move towards pleasure and away from pain, both the Sun's and Venus' entry into Scorpio remind us that when we relax from rigidly held appetites and aversions, we can mine the medicine in every moment – breaking the good–bad binary to become even more.

0

Saturn stations direct in Aquarius

WE CAN BE HEROES: Since Saturn's April slowdown, we've been asked to look at where we compartmentalize our self-expression – believing that only some parts of us are fit for particular forums. With this planet of self-sufficient growth now heading forwards for the rest of the year, it's time for some serious soul-stretching, as we let our self-concepts become even more limber. This starts with a commitment to **engage in everyday acts of heroism – championing the feats we accomplish, no matter how minute**, and using our sweet little superpowers to beckon us beyond so-called safety. You are wider and wilder than you believe. With this astro event, it's game on for catapulting yourself over the vault of any self-imposed blocks.

New Moon in Scorpio
(partial solar eclipse)

PRESENT FOR THE PASSING: We often want to leap straight for the next lustrous thing – bouncing back gamely after life's messy break-ups instead of tending to what hurts. But with celestial surgeon Scorpio running the show and the Sun's light partially blocked, this cosmic event asks us to **rip off the temporary bandages and forgo superficial strategies in order to truly reset the broken**

bones beneath. Whether or not you feel like you're in the throes of an intense 'death' moment, you can use this Moon to uncover whatever you might have previously composted without full consideration – harnessing its strong, tonifying medicine to help you deal with it now rather than later. Standing vigil for whatever arises will mean you can turn towards the next thing when it's actually time, allowing you to move forward from a place of empowered integration rather than having a fractured reaction.

Mars stations retrograde in Gemini
(stations direct on 12 January 2023)

SWEETS BEFORE SUPPER: Mars in Gemini diversifies our sources of engine-revving inspo, and with the planet now slowing down for the rest of the year, it's **an invite to expand our concepts of action and inaction.** Begin by noticing when you commend yourself for driven efforts, or chastise yourself for laziness. Just like the courageous cells turning over in your body, or the under-the-soil preparations of nature, there's always something happening, even if it appears off camera. Soften any rigid attempts at striking a perfect work–life balance, or having to put in the work to get out the reward. Find flow in the midst of professional madness and a sense of accomplishment while stretched out on the sun lounger, and give yourself permission to pop a few sweet treats before supper.

0

STAR PARTY:
ECLIPSE SEASON PART TWO
(25 OCTOBER–8 NOVEMBER)

Part deux of the Taurus/Scorpio eclipse party rages
on. While the April–May eclipse energies asked us
to banish scarcity mentality by building full-bodied
faith in the endless buffet of birthing, this second
round invites us to combat 'lack' at the other end
of the spectrum – uncovering trust by dancing with
the emptiness of dying. But before you let that send
you diving under the covers in fright, feel into the
spaciousness that can come from absence. Cartwheel
through the cavernous gaps as you await your next refill.

SIGN-BY-SIGN
GUIDE TO OCTOBER

♎ LIBRA

Happy birth time, little light sabre! October is your moment to lift yourself straight up to the clouds – applying your evolutionary capacity to elevate life beyond its current humdrum condition with both friendliness and force. Start by homing in on whatever you want to breathe beauty into and using your clear seeing to strip away the excess. Maybe it's a complicated conversation that can be simplified with a couple of bold statements, or a dream that's been ready for hatching but just needs fewer strings attached to bring it into existence. Trust that you can find serenity in selecting the most essential elements and raising them up like a paper airplane – elegantly aerodynamic and ready to fly.

✦ With this October's emphasis on the heavy-hitting signs of Aries, Scorpio and Capricorn, it's time to embrace a little grit alongside your glamour. Notice where you might have backed down from believing yourself on an issue that's near and dear to your heart – perhaps thinking that you don't have the right to a rallying cry. While your toughness might not always feel as tangible as some of the flashier zodiac fighters, you are here to show us that endurance can be artful. Raise your sabre like a queen and step into the fray with self-possessed poise.

♏ SCORPIO

Originally joined as one sign in a single constellation, Libra and Scorpio exist at the frontline of intimacy. They're here to show us what life can be when we accept it all. Borrow some of Libra's grace to polish your deep dives. You can re-centre from anything, reeling yourself back to the surface with a calm, loving hand if it gets too sticky.

+ With a potent eclipse in your sign this month, remember the 'hands on' power of your hot-blooded healing presence. You can endure so much more than the rest of us, and this can feel like a strong, spacious gift rather than a burden.

♐ SAGITTARIUS

Here to explore the land between the real and the possible, Libra and Sagittarius are on a meaningful mission. This month, borrow a bit of Libra's calibration consciousness, considering the potential impact of your power moves, both on yourself and others, taking care to hit your target without causing burnout.

+ With Mercury direct and Venus in conversation with your ruler, Jupiter, use your over-the-top risk tolerance to ignite a love light in others, becoming a self-acceptance coach as you share wherever your heart is at without equivocating.

♑ CAPRICORN

Two cool kids who understand the value of a little refined restraint, both Libra and Capricorn model the majesty that's possible when we gather ourselves to centre. This month, let Libra's pastel palette help you smooth any rough edges of severity – reminding yourself that effortless elegance is utterly badass.

✦ With Pluto in your sign now rolling direct, exercise the muscle of your inner authority with ease and grace – noticing wherever you've outsourced your power and taking back your rightful seat in the boss's office with organic ownership.

♒ AQUARIUS

Wise beyond belief, both Libra and Aquarius have a prophetic power to glimpse the endgame while still in motion. Borrow bits of Libra's art of alignment and equilibrium this month, as you explore releasing some of your attachment to outcomes in favour of a game-time manoeuvring that lets you respond to the terrain as it is right now.

✦ With Saturn stationing direct in your sign, remind yourself just how much people need you. While you can sometimes feel 'exiled' by your out-there notions, let this month be an invite back into the mix – forging alliances with those who celebrate you, strange sides and all.

♓ PISCES

The crystal-clear cloud puff to your gauzy soft-lit sensations, Libra's dream-weaving lifts Piscean visions out from the invisible and into 3-D. Take October to champion this concretizing process as you silence any fears that tell you it cannot be done. Commit to bringing your highest hopes from being mere nocturnal notions into the light of day, even if it means compromising some of their contours.

✦ As Jupiter prepares to retrograde back into your sign, examine any metaphorical clothing that feels constrictive. If it's itchy, scratchy or in any way stifling, swap those old threads for a new sartorial situation that allows ample room to move and groove.

♈ ARIES

Existing on a polarity playing field together, Aries and Libra are both fearless champions of rising up and flying forwards on the wings of a courageous cause. Let Libra's *pas de deux* infuse your power moves with the power of two – letting any places you're holding to a single vision come into communion with the other side.

0

✦ As Jupiter temporarily backs out of your sign from the end of this month through mid-December, it's a soft-lit moment for balancing friction with fusion. How could an opportunity for expansion feel as easy-breezy as a long outbreath?

♉ TAURUS

Ruled by the petal power of Venus, Libra is the civilized curator to the more rustic pursuits of Taurus. Take this month to remember that you don't always have to accept things exactly as they are. Power up with the possibility of actively shaping and augmenting your reality to make it more in line with what you actually need.

✦ With a Scorpio eclipse kicking off part two of this year's cycle in your pair of signs, don't fear the reaper – trust that abundant blooms will spring from fallow ground, and rely on storehouses of spiritual sustenance to combat any scarcity.

♊ GEMINI

Light-footed luminaries who sample the wares and adjust accordingly, both Libra and Gemini are here to explore life's dualities and seeming contradictions. Harness some of Libra's call to weigh the options and make a choice – simply selecting whatever pathway glows brightest without stressing over any roads not taken.

+ With Mars in your sign rolling retrograde through the year's end, draw your life force back to centre, remembering that you are the sole director of your own experience and trusting in your inventive genius to devise unexpected solutions to old problems.

♋ CANCER

Libra is the cool-headed collaborator to Cancer's more covetous companion, and is here to teach the crab about a love that is equal parts unwavering affection and mutual admiration. Let October be an invite to explore respectful adoration, allowing whatever warms your heart to have a right to its own wants.

+ With a pair of intensely charged Moons in Aries and Scorpio this month, let any vigorous feelings that flow through your system become purifying rather than overwhelming, as you embrace the supercharge of even the strongest sensations.

♌ LEO

A pair of emboldened beauticians who cherish what 'could be', Libra and Leo are both here to keep the bubbly flowing. Take October to balance your self-led mission to love this life with the ability to let it love you back, allowing any passion projects to be equal parts personally penned and communally inspired.

+ As Saturn stations direct in your opposite sign of Aquarius, consider the long-term effects of your causes, easing up on any impassioned fights or energetic output that's breaking your body down rather than building up your bones.

♍ VIRGO

A curatorial pair of cosmic companions who riff on the natural goodness of life and make it even better, both Libra and Virgo assess the alignment between inner and outer resources at every turn. Borrow some of Libra's Cardinal action this month, trusting that you have every right to claim your role as landscape architect of your own life.

+ As Mercury makes its final direct station of the year in your sign, it's a potent moment for integrating and processing your experiences. Don't be afraid to press pause, move at your own pace and allow ample time to absorb the after-effects of any actions taken.

STAR STYLE

COLOUR: Cut through the noise with sophisticated, clear-headed shades, ballerina pastels, impressionistic hues and Malibu tones. Think soft greys, refined aquas and violets, camera-ready sunsets, pitch black and pure white, icy mints, slipper pinks and navy.

FASHION: Elevate your aesthetics with French New Wave and royal bridal shower inspo. Think clean lines, classic cool, simple trench coats, white satin, velvet brocade, peplum blazers, empire waists, windswept scarves, bell sleeves, tights and ballet flats, casual culottes and finessed florals. No matter what your sartorial selection, play with contrast and comparison in your ensemble, as in colour blocking: tough leather with soft lace, and old-meets-new.

SCENT: October's aromas are carefully curated bouquets, clarifying citruses and equilibrating extractions. Think orchids, grapefruit, mint, synergistic essential oil blends and fragrant diffusers that uplift the everyday environment.

FOOD FOR THE SOUL

Enjoy delicious candied confections, perfect pairings and epicurean presentations, such as sparkling water with garnishes, sweet and salty snacks, scones with cream, black-and-white cookies, French macarons and madeleines, honey and lemon, and pressed panini.

O

CHART YOUR COURSE

October's energies invite us to coherently and transparently assess our lives as they are, so we can birth them into what they might be. Champion clarity with jaunts to lands that finesse the finite and lift humanity up to a high art. Think Greek temples, Florentine palazzos, Austrian coffee houses, Argentine tangos and Abu Dhabi cosmopolitanism. Closer to home, harmonize your habitat with indoor–outdoor living, trips to local monuments, architectural tours and clarifying walks under your corner of the sky.

ELEMENTAL EXCURSIONS

Cardinal Air-sign-ruled October is customized for cultured evenings, high-minded musings and anything that's energetically and aesthetically balancing. Think gallery expeditions, figure-drawing classes, photography lessons, jazz ensembles, ballroom dancing, topiary garden wandering, debates, intellectual salons and hot/cold saunas.

PLANETARY PROMPTS

Use these magic words and journal
questions to moor you this month…

CLARITY:

What realities need facing right now?

RECONCILIATION:

What do I think of as 'not mine' that bears examination?

SYNERGY:

What can I change and what is beyond my control;
how can I better partner with the forces in my life?

EQUILIBRIUM:

How do I feel into my own sense of
'rightness' when making decisions?

ELEVATION:

How can I distinguish between my true
dreams and desires and the 'shoulds'?

O

MONDAY	TUESDAY	WEDNESDAY	THURSDAY	FRIDAY	SATURDAY	SUNDAY
	8 NOVEMBER Full Moon in Taurus (total lunar eclipse)			**11 NOVEMBER** Sun in Scorpio square Saturn in Aquarius		
		16 NOVEMBER Venus enters Sagittarius	**17 NOVEMBER** Mercury enters Sagittarius			
	22 NOVEMBER Sun enters Sagittarius	**23 NOVEMBER** Jupiter stations direct in Pisces New Moon in Sagittarius				

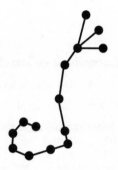

NOVEMBER

GLOW IN THE DARK

GLOW IN THE DARK

The heart of November's astrology beats in the dead of night and underneath the sheets. A time for bumping and grinding with all that lives in the belly of our beasts, this month's questions hang courageously charged in the air: how far will you go? How deep is your love?

Urged onwards by the eighth sign of Scorpio, November asks us to forge a pact with the totality of our human experience – forgoing being nice for getting good and real. After October's Libran emphasis on aligned equilibrium, we are ready to go harder, as we reconcile and reunite with the parts we usually hide from sight. This is a sign that penetrates below the ground with a headlamp and scalpel – there are no half measures for surgeon Scorpio. This is all-or-nothing territory. And its intensity is born from a simple, startling revelation: we are mortal, and everything ends in the end.

Ruled by the Tarot's Death card itself, November is where we awaken to our expiration date and are asked to reckon with the anticipation of this ending. Once we're reacquainted with the reality of our assured demise, our aliveness glows even stronger and brighter. A life that is finite is a life that's worth living, and November's cosmic energies want us to remember this.

Notoriously associated with sex and death, representing its innate animalism, Scorpio asks us to bring consciousness to our carnality this month. Symbolized by the scorpion, the snake, the eagle and the phoenix, Scorpio energy is both break-it-down-to-dirt composter and soul survivor, here to embrace the entirety of the jungle experience. Both a till-death-do-us-part and a beyond-the-grave moment, November is a month to take our natural place within the life/death/rebirth cycle, and in doing so uncover the unbreakable, immortal molten core within us that can never be destroyed.

Dually ruled by Mars and Pluto, which govern both our innate life force and the forces that act upon us, Scorpio reminds us that when we come at life completely, we find out what we're made of. And when we let life come at us, beyond fear, we discover that there is really never anything to lose. In a land where nothing is left out, we find the strength for transformation that springs not from an urge to fix but from a fierce forgiveness, which blesses ourselves and our fellow humans in all our beautiful beastliness. We all come from the same place, and we're all headed back there, too – intimately bound by the shared desire to live to the fullest while we're here.

Give this month your tired and your weak, your burned-out, your bottomed-out and your way-beyond-the-pale parts. The desires you don't even dare to whisper about. The things you try to swallow down. Let it rise and lay it all at November's feet.

N

NOVEMBER DATES WITH
DESTINY: THE OPEN ROAD

With our yearly eclipse party drawing to a close in Scorpio's opposite sign of Taurus, expansive Jupiter stationing direct in feel-it-to-heal-it Pisces, and a flurry of planets entering the wild pony pastures of Sagittarius, **November is a month to loosen your grip – noticing where and how you 'block' yourself, and why, and committing to taking a riskier road going forwards.** Combined with Scorpio's capacity to dive deep and stay with perceived discomfort, start by noticing where you might be standing in the way of your own evolution and any fears that are keeping you stuck. Maybe it's a habit pattern you keep reaching for, even though it feels hollow. Or a self-incriminating storyline that swirls constantly in your brain. Be tender with these places but also tough, as you practise setting these fears to the side each time they arise and carrying on less encumbered.

Full Moon in Taurus
(total lunar eclipse)

BIG IS BEAUTIFUL: Our final phase of the Taurus–Scorpio eclipse cycle that began back in April, this lustrous astral event – which picks up a special glow from the synergy between the Earth, Sun and Moon – is a no-holds-barred harvest that asks us to uncover the potential pleasure in all of life's platters by welcoming whatever arrives on our table. **Notice what happens when you let a certain emotion intensify, no matter what its 'flavour'.** Maybe it's anger that you let build to a full-blown rage, only to discover that when it's totally and completely unleashed, it becomes pure exhilaration. Or a tender desire, that when tended to unwaveringly also reveals some bittersweet sadness beneath that wants your amorous attention. When you let things blossom into their unbridled bigness, you may be surprised by the flowers you find.

Sun in Scorpio square Saturn in Aquarius

ROCK N' ROLL: Scorpio and Aquarius are the zodiac's raw and ready renegades. Both Fixed sign deep divers, they are here to excavate the surface and overturn old orders. As the planetary powerhouses of the Sun and Saturn interlock in these signs, it's a time to hang

N

tough and celebrate your survival skills, remembering that getting tumbled through life's ups and downs can provide precious emotional experience rather than punishment. How can you reclaim the beastier bits of your story and learn to sport your so-called scars as part of the cosmic contouring of your irreplaceable shape? Adopt a live-and-let-live approach to life's down and dirtier moments, viewing them as vivid opportunities to remember your very own aliveness. You're still here. And you get to feel it all.

Venus enters Sagittarius

YOUR LOVE IS WILD: An open plain of passion – when pleasure-seeker Venus transits the sign of the bareback pony, heaven breaks loose on earth. This planetary passage helps us brush past small hurts, to let ourselves and others be freer and wilder with our love. In all kinds of relationships, **take this time to explore what you're asking of others – the limits and walls of expectation you put up.** While you don't have to completely destroy your boundaries or dumb down your standards, could you honestly investigate which of these are actually crafted from love and respect for self and others, and which spring from fear of getting left behind or being the one on the so-called losing side? This transit reminds us that there are really no losers in life, and that each heart opening towards another human is a win for the spirit.

17

Mercury enters Sagittarius

THE MEANING OF LIFE: When the metamorphic magic of Mercury entangles with Sagittarius' majestic mane, it's a moment to **start asking bigger questions and learning to live in the expansive ellipses of 'what if?'** Like a child learning the word 'why' for the very first time, start to question any and all assumed parts of your life from a place of curiosity rather than aggression. Why is your day ordered in a certain way? Why do you feel like you have to play particular roles? Why can't you choose differently this time? Imagine that you're hosting a foreign visitor to your world and explain each custom and choice – notice where the reasoning might be in want of an upgrade and use this process of revision to uncover what actually has lasting meaning for your life.

22

Sun enters Sagittarius

NOTHING LEFT TO LOSE: This is one of the most unfettered cosmic shifts of the year. **Once we've reached the bottom of Scorpio season, we've got nothing to do but fly.** Both of these signs' energies help us build trust, with Scorpio bringing us up against fear to find our forever footing and Sagittarius stoking our faith and courageously coming alive to a new adventure. Use this shift to consider where you've been pushed to the limit, directly confronted with something sticky that you didn't think you could face. What's on the other side of this limit? Do you feel buoyant and ready for boldness? Or in need of rest and rejuvenation before you roll the dice once again? Wherever you find yourself, take some delight in the clearing, like an open field just beginning to twinkle with life after a torrential storm.

Jupiter stations direct in Pisces

LET IT BE: Jupiter's retrograde roll, which started at the end of July, has taken it from fiery forceful Aries back into the Piscean waters of allowing, and this transition asks us to find more trust in our inevitable expansions, even when they appear less visible to the naked eye. Take this time to explore where the art of allowing could create more 'width' in your life; practise giving parts of your existence more room to move and morph of their own accord. Maybe it's pressing pause on a project for a few days and letting a new approach bubble up. Or taking time and space from a relationship without its having to signal a decisive 'end'. Letting your hard lines get a little fuzzy and **leaving life to its own devices can allow solutions to arise without you having to exhaust your resources searching for them.**

23

New Moon in Sagittarius

THIS OR BETTER: A courageous co-creator with the wild trip that is life, Sagittarius energy's highest good is reached when we take our hands off the wheel and let goddess intervene. Where do you feel like you already have all the answers, as though it's a done deal that's signed, sealed and delivered? **When we try to control, define or know it all, we refuse our numinous guides the right to do their job**, which is assisting in the spaces we leave for them and lifting us towards lands we couldn't even have imagined if we'd attempted to map all the contours ourselves. No matter your spiritual proclivities, use this Moon to imagine that even your 'best' work and brightest dreams could be enhanced by showing a little faith – undoing the ties on your packages and letting life have a go at gifting you something even better.

STAR PARTY:
SAMHAIN (1 NOVEMBER)

The witchiest cross-quarter holiday on the Pagan Wheel of the Year – starting on the eve of 31 October and running through 1 November – Samhain, which coincides with Mexico's Day of the Dead and the Christian All Saints' Day, lifts the veil on the layers between life here on earth and the 'other' side. But rather than facing a frightful confrontation with the underworld, traditional celebrants took this time to lay out a feast for these forces. Even trick-or-treating began with door-to-door travels to sing songs of the dead.

SIGN-BY-SIGN
GUIDE TO NOVEMBER

♏ SCORPIO

Happy birth time, precious phoenix! November is a rich opportunity to bring yourself back to the centre, filling up fiercely on the concept of 'possession'. Start by looking at where you long to possess something outside of yourself, or where you feel like you get taken over by forces beyond your control. Draw these feelings in as though you're sporting a perfectly tailored, cinched-waist outfit – become a self-possessed mistress of your own longings whose power simmers and builds and even finds beauty in some badass brooding. You're often described as being intense, but what you sometimes forget is that intensity is simply evidence of your unabashed lust for life. When you relish this intensity instead of repressing it, your power grows from the inside. Let this month be a homecoming to your natural-born magnetism.

✦ As Neptune meets up with your honorary ruler, Lilith, consider the power of sheer imagination. Notice the electrical charge and energetic heat created by envisioning what you long for – the craving that runs wild and finds its own way through the world when it isn't constrained by the pressure of having to 'get'. Whatever you're wishing for longs to have a life of its own this month, without your having to control its unfolding. Forgo five-year plans for pure feral fantasy.

♐ SAGITTARIUS

The scuba diver to Sagittarius' desert wanderer, Scorpio brings extra depth to the wild pony's longings. November is your opportunity to go fully 'down and in', focusing your force on something without dispersing it. Even if you're just locking eyes with a beloved for an extra second, letting it 'stick' builds extra strength.

✦ With your ruler, Jupiter, stationing direct and a pack of planets entering your sign, it's an existential moment for remembering why you came into the world in the first place. Don't be afraid to ask the big questions and live in the space between Q and A.

♑ CAPRICORN

Two soul survivors here to embrace eternity, both Scorpio and Capricorn are endurance experts of the first order. Let November be an invitation to fuse your calm-headed, mature soul magic with some feral force, as you revel in the battle of life itself. Remember that sometimes the things worth wanting are worth fighting for.

✦ With the Sun, Mercury and Venus squaring off against your ruler, Saturn, consider where you could swap 'expert' knowledge for experiential learning, forgoing asking others and letting your own life on the ground teach you.

N

♒ AQUARIUS

A pair of mystical mavericks who delight in being contrary, Scorpio and Aquarius are here to rebel with a cause. Let Scorpio's rawness lead you back to the heart of your belief systems this month, as you work it for your world view – remembering that claiming your right to live in exactly the way you want never needs to be justified.

✦ As the Sun, Mercury and Venus oppose your ruler Uranus, consider the 'tiny' revolutions that occur on a daily basis, seizing micro-opportunities to embrace the changes you're craving and shaking it up on a second-by-second basis.

♓ PISCES

The hot-blooded steam to Piscean ethereal mists, Scorpio is here to teach the little mermaid about the primal power of love. Use November to embrace the telekinetic potency of your desires. Rather than closing your eyes and hoping it will one day come true, lock eyes with what you want across a crowded room and draw it to you like a magnet.

✦ With Jupiter now rolling direct through your sign, assess what in your life wants to be left alone and what wants to be consciously buffed. You'll know the difference from the mental effort required – anything that 'hurts your brain' wants to sort itself without your interference.

♈ ARIES

Tough tendrils ever unfurling towards life, both Scorpio and Aries exist on the front lines. Get an extra carnal charge from Scorpio's 'never say die' attitude this month, taking November as an opportunity to up the ante on your loyalty to a cause, as you let seeing it past the finishing line become your fiercest flex.

◆ With your ruler, Mars, travelling retrograde for its first full month, explore hidden opportunities and tucked-in pockets of energy. Forgo any fixed schedules for the buoyancy of ebbing and flowing with your force as you feel it in each moment.

♉ TAURUS

The bestial feaster that devours Taurus' buttered bread, Scorpio is here to teach the bovine beauty about trusting life's ability to serve up seconds at the buffet. Let November be an exercise in drinking existence right to the bottom without feeling bottomed out – imbibing whatever cups present themselves without fear of running out.

N

✦ This month's final Full Moon eclipse in your sign is an epic opportunity to harvest the fruits of your efforts. What is ripe on the vine and ready for plucking? Don't waste a moment assessing whether to wait a little longer – just get juicing.

♊ GEMINI

The butterfly wings to Scorpio's spelunking rope, Gemini can learn from the scorpion's ability to journey beneath the surface and hang out with whatever stalactites can be found. Take November to push yourself up against a limit – staying on just past the point where things start to get sticky and seeing what gemstones can be mined in this fixity.

✦ With Mars spending its first full month retrograding through your sign, learn to 'read' your energy levels fluently. Feel into your own particular circadian rhythms without their having to sync with external expectations about productivity.

♋ CANCER

The down-and-dirty den to Cancer's living room sofa, Scorpio is here to offer the crab the empowered emotional prowess that lives in the country beyond comfort zones. Take some emotional risks in November, releasing whatever you're gripping solely in the name of so-called security and finding a new shell that better fits your growing spirit.

✦ With this month's New Moon and Full Moon unfolding in Taurus and Sagittarius – two signs with an appetite for more – explore your own concept of 'too much'. Notice where you limit or restrict your longings and let yourself indulge instead.

♌ LEO

Two magic meat-lovers who are here to dig into the heart of the matter, Leo and Scorpio find exuberant enjoyment in going over the top. Glow in the dark this November, trusting that your sun-kissed sparkle is vital even in the toughest times, as you shine your heart's headlight and remain present for whatever gets illuminated.

✦ With this month's emphasis on fellow Fixed signs Taurus and Scorpio, explore your relationship to 'staying with' your life, imagining that you were attending the bedside of a beloved, and holding space for the entirety of experience.

♍ VIRGO

Two existential exorcists who draw the excess to the surface and divine what really counts, Scorpio and Virgo are both here to assess exactly what's worth the investment. Take sharp-eyed stock of your storehouse this month – letting your gut instinct guide you to know the difference between what's good and what's ready to go.

✦ As your ruler, Mercury, meets up with a flurry of outer planets, it's a time to forgo the trees for the forest. Release yourself from the urge to get caught up in the weedy details of a situation, and embrace the overarching meaning instead.

♎ LIBRA

Originally part of the same sign, both Scorpio and Libra share a penchant for reflection and reconciliation – getting intimate with each piece to bless the nature of our human whole. Borrow a bit of Scorpio's more self-contained prowess this month, forgoing some of your compassionate consideration of outside forces to tap into the passionate force within.

✦ With the year's final eclipse in fellow Venus-ruled Taurus, take time to rest on your luscious laurels, considering where you might be holding back from excitement out of self-critique and choosing to celebrate your success instead.

STAR STYLE

COLOUR: Embrace the hues that come alive after sunset, such as macabre shades fit for Cleopatra, unearthed geodes and glow-in-the-dark bioluminescent tones. Think blood rubies, neon magentas, oxblood, oxidized metallics, black glitter, classic kohl and burned liquid gold.

FASHION: Survive in style with a bulletproof 1970s Bond girl meets Roman bacchanal look. Think bodysuits, plunging zippers, louche loungewear, daring cut-outs, strong shoulders, garter belts, serpentine bracelets and thigh-high vinyl boots. And whatever you wear, find the 'core' of your look – a ring that you never take off, boots you have resoled for resiliency, or weatherproof materials that protect your power.

SCENT: November's aromas are heady, nocturnal and composed of both compost and blossoms. Think tuberose, oud, ashes, jasmine, neroli, funereal lily and the scent of your own sweat-drenched, living skin.

FOOD FOR THE SOUL

Dig into midnight snacks, seafood treats and primitive palate-cleansers like unpitted olives, black cherries, prime cut rare steak, shark meat, ghost pepper, rock candy and after-dinner digestifs.

N

CHART YOUR COURSE

November's energies ask us to chart a course through our mortal coil and also our immortal core. Uncover all that's hidden with trips to ancient sites and underground haunts. Think the catacombs of Paris, Cappadocia's cave hotels, the Egyptian pyramids, the hedonistic jazz clubs of New Orleans and deserts after dark. Closer to home, explore subway transit and railway tunnels, enjoy a celebration in a cemetery, where life goes on despite its limits, or play with planning a 'last day on Earth' – letting your intensive itinerary take you to all of your desired dens before nightfall.

ELEMENTAL EXCURSIONS

Fixed Water-sign-ruled November is built for going harder, deeper and longer, as we push beyond the superficial to find out what really makes us tick. Think scuba diving, escape room adventures, basement cleanouts, mud wrestling, archaeological digs, depth therapy, strength training, detective novels and unsolved mysteries.

PLANETARY PROMPTS

Use these magic words and journal
questions to moor you this month…

EXCAVATION:

What scares me the most and why?

POWER:

How can I distinguish between grasping for
control and exercising my strength?

FORGIVENESS:

If I knew I had very little time left, how might
I treat myself and others differently?

MORTALITY/IMMORTALITY:

Where am I currently in the life/death/rebirth cycle,
and what remains 'eternal' no matter what?

TRANSFORMATION:

What am I ready to actively lay down on
the fire, and what can I let die?

N

MONDAY	TUESDAY	WEDNESDAY	THURSDAY	FRIDAY	SATURDAY	SUNDAY
						4 DECEMBER Neptune stations direct in Pisces
	6 DECEMBER Mercury enters Capricorn		**8 DECEMBER** Full Moon in Gemini		**10 DECEMBER** Venus enters Capricorn	
		21 DECEMBER Sun enters Capricorn		**23 DECEMBER** New Moon in Capricorn Chiron stations direct in Aries		

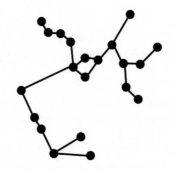

DECEMBER

ONWARDS

ONWARDS

Racing down the track with mane unfurled, December's astrology is boundlessly energetic, stretching its muscular legs to meet the turf. A month for flexing our faith and turning it loose to the rhythm of the Divine, December's call comes at us saddled up ready for the rollicking ride ahead. The open-ended question of the month ahead: Do you believe that life is on your side?

Ruled by the ninth sign of Sagittarius, December invites us to join the cosmic conga line with overflowing goblet in hand. After November's Scorpionic deep dives, we've got nothing left to lose and more than enough room to move, having faced our fears and freed ourselves from them. An invitation to laugh and learn through each lusty experience, December reminds us that life always moves towards more life, and encourages us to revel in our vitality until our very last breath. This month wants you to become positively plus-sized – bigging up the parts of your life that already glitter and amplifying the glimmers just arriving on the horizon.

December is our chance to adopt a little casino consciousness – a time for 'backing' ourselves by believing that life, in turn, will have our backs. Risk tolerance is our rainbow jet fuel this month, and it's a time to liberate limits and dismantle doubts, ditching any weighty baggage that might delay take-off. Like a rip-roaring red convertible road trip taken at top speed, December can joyously 'unstick' the parts of your life that are ready to be let loose.

In the Tarot, Sagittarius is guided by the Temperance card, a heaven-sent mover and shaker who reminds us that we cannot do it all on our own. Following November's face-to-face encounter with the fireproof parts of our power that can never be melted down, in December's Sagittarius country we are asked to fire up our faith in a higher power – so secure in our right to life that we can lighten our hold on the outcomes.

However you envisage the Divine, it's a month for easing your grip on the 'how' and letting each wondrous unfolding in your day become a scavenger-hunt clue from the Universe, leading you ever closer to your 'why'. December's magic medicine is found in the seeking as much as in the finding. It asks us to swap 'knowing it all' for the wild notion that our own lives might know even better.

Take December to untie your life from the hitching posts of hesitation and to celebrate your sheer existence with head held high towards the spacious sky. Your story is still being written, penned equally by the gorgeous go-getter within you and by goddess herself. The world is wild. The runway is wide. Wheels up...

DECEMBER DATES WITH DESTINY: JUST DO YOU

Competent Capricorn planets are joining the Sagittarius party this month, with dreamy Neptune finding its forward-rolling footing and Jupiter sparking it up in Aries once again. December is therefore a month to remember that, no matter where we are and how we feel about it all, **we can find solace by summoning the strength to show up to live the lives that only we can live.** Start by noticing where you might be looking at another person's paper for the answers, following their progress closely and comparing it with your own. While there's nothing wrong with finding inspiration outside yourself, this month is made for making your own way first. Think of little kids on the beach, unleashed onto the sand and intuitively knowing their 'role' – whether they're the ones gathering water, digging the holes or decorating the sandcastles with seashells. What's asking to be done right now that only you can do? Show up in service of your singularity and shine on.

4

Neptune stations direct in Pisces

SELF-GIVEN SALVATION: Neptune's retrograde roll since the end of June has been an opportunity to take charge of our own dreams – no longer waiting for a saviour to fashion our fantasy suite and plumping our own pillows instead. Now the planet's forward motion smokes out any narratives around helplessness, empowering us to lay claim, without a trace of blame, to where we've been wounded. While there is certainly value in holding ourselves and others accountable for actions taken, there is also majestic medicine in letting go of a checks-and-balances accounting of our anguish. Explore where you might be 'stuck' with the belief that a piece of the past must be righted before you can move on. There is no closure in this life, except for the solace we're able to gift ourselves. **Let the knowledge that no one and nothing can 'wrap it up' for you with a tidy bow be a wild chance to release any hardness around a hurt.**

Mercury enters Capricorn
(stations retrograde on 29th)

COMMEMORATE THE WEIGHT: As light-footed Mercury completes its tour through all 12 signs and returns to Capricorn's gorgeous gravity field, where it was at the end of January, it's high time to hail the heft of our life experiences. Mercury in Capricorn slows our nervous system and ups the ante on the importance of our experiences – asking us to consider how every step contributes to the endgame. Start by exploring whatever might be pressing on you, letting any feelings of overwhelm at the sheer weight of the world rise without critique. Lay your body down on the ground, put your hands on any place that feels heavy, and **remember that you deserve to be a part of this planet – affecting and affected by life's changes.** When you sink into the deep grooves of gravity without turning away, you can come back to your own weight and worth in gold.

Full Moon in Gemini

THE SCHOOL OF LIFE: The astrological axis of Gemini and Sagittarius asks us to apprentice ourselves to life – laying claim to what we know as we know it and simultaneously letting these beliefs remain buoyant and breathable as they respond to the ever-changing intel of our life experience. This Gemini Full Moon is **an invitation to home in on an area of life where we think we've 'graduated' and enrol in a little postgraduate study instead.** Attend to anywhere you've become a broken record, repeating a belief that feels like it verges on personal plagiarism. Releasing yourself from having to endlessly perform an old song allows you to expand your voice and perspective in service of a new hit single.

Venus enters Capricorn

THE HEART GOES ON: With Venus' journey through the signs also complete, returning to Capricorn for the first time since early March, we've learned a lot about our love stories – examining how we become available to receive the good stuff, our standards for sweetness and our capacity for softness. Whatever your partnership status and passionate proclivities, use this transit to honour the times when you've opened up to life, no matter how wide or narrow. In the face of your entire life history – the bitter twists and the honeyed turns – look at just how far you've come. You may long to trust more. You may yearn to connect more deeply. But just take a minute to consider that **your heart is exactly where it should be and it's doing just fine** – still here, beating on and able, whenever it's ready, to reach out once again.

Sun enters Capricorn

EVERYTHING MATTERS: This is the calendar year's cosmic birthday, when the Sun's ingress back into Capricorn brings us full circle on the zodiac wheel. And just like any legacy-laden toast, **it's a time to raise our glasses to the sky and remember that our experience here on Earth is nothing if not remarkable.** Feel into your battle scars. Your soft places and your hardened layers. The whole story of you that is deposited in your beautiful body and walks with you through every moment of the day. No need to apologize for what moves you, for what matters most to you or for how much it matters. Take this transition as your licence to let yourself be counted – unafraid to consider the stately significance and consequence of all the days you've lived and the years you've still got left.

New Moon in Capricorn

INVISIBLE LINES: Harkening back to the 2 January Capricorn New Moon, this lunar event brings us home, giving us **a chance to consider how well the lines we've drawn are serving our sense of self.** Explore how and why you've been defending parts of your life, noticing where erecting a barrier feels creatively supportive and where it has become stifling. Is there a border you've been policing not out of pleasure but out of fear that you don't actually have the power to protect it? Could letting in a little of life reveal that your capacity to defend your honour is self-sustaining without your having to stressfully show someone where that boundary is? Like the distinction between a paper map of countries and the land viewed from above, let your lines become less visible but no less real.

Chiron stations direct in Aries

ASTONISH YOURSELF: Retrograde since mid-July, Chiron's slowdown asked us to claim our birthright to just 'be' – remembering that showing up, head high and spine straight, is all that's really required of us. With the planetoid now gearing up for forward motion, **consider how you might bring extra awareness to the wonder that is you** – witnessing yourself from an almost out-of-body perspective. While this may sound trippy at first, rather than a chance to critique your every move, let it feel like an opportunity to adopt an attitude of awe. Just as you'd watch a beloved cross the room at a crowded party, could you commit to marvelling at the way you move through your own life?

STAR PARTY:
SOLSTICE (21 DECEMBER)

Following the Cancer-ruled comforts of the 21 June solstice, this second solstice – the winter solstice in the northern hemisphere, the summer solstice in the southern hemisphere – occurs in the stately sign of Capricorn. Watched over by The Devil and The World Tarot cards, it's a time for exercising our right to belong wherever we are. When you let yourself relax into your physical and energetic body – taking the natural shape of 'you' without holding back – you fit more organically into the world at large.

SIGN-BY-SIGN
GUIDE TO DECEMBER

↗ SAGITTARIUS

Happy birth month, wild pony! A bareback ride through the beauties of bigness, December is your chance to work on all forms of expansion. Begin by assessing where you might benefit from just doing whatever needs to be done on a regular basis so that the lucky wheel of life can spin all on its own. Treating it like a surprise party that the Universe is planning just for you, leave the house for a walkabout while the celebration gets prepped. And where are you ready to toss something to the heavens that you can't handle alone any more? Turn it loose at every turn, leaving room for life to show how much it loves you.

+ With Jupiter primed to re-enter Aries, this month might feel like the final contraction before the expansion that births the baby. Remember, there's no need to fear any perceived setbacks. Instead, hold space for anything you might be forcing out of the car because you're afraid it'll make a grab for the wheel and lead you back to a land you'd rather leave in the dust. Trust that your ever-expanding self is firmly in the driver's seat and that there's nothing that needs to be forcibly left behind for you to get ahead.

♑ CAPRICORN

The celebratory whoosh of wind that pushes the mountain goat onward, Sagittarius is here to bring buoyancy to Capricorn's serious soul mission. Let December be your invite to catch air wherever it can be found – persisting with less resistance and using the natural momentum that's already at play to support your endeavours.

✦ With a holy trinity of planets coming home to your sign, it's a magic moment for returning to yourself. Rein in anywhere you've been overextending towards others and step back into your boudoir for a little self-indulging staycation.

♒ AQUARIUS

Both wild and free babes born to push past the limits, Sagittarius and Aquarius are built to break on through to the other side. This month, borrow some of Sagittarius' goddess-given grab-and-go spontaneity to add to your more strategic mix, and get carried away by the immersive experience of living without needing to 'know'.

✦ With a meet-up this month between your ruler, Uranus, and sweetheart Venus, release your grip on how the good stuff comes to you, allowing yourself to find beauty in pleasure packages of all shapes and sizes.

♓ PISCES

Faith-based healers here to let it go and turn it loose, Pisces and Sagittarius share a direct dial to the Divine. Embrace Sagittarius' big vision this month, as you remember your right to lay claim to your vital role in any 'wins'. Even if you were assisted by all manner of angels, it was still you at the centre of the heavenly chorus.

✦ With your ruler, Neptune, now direct in your sign, stage your own ceremony for anything that's asking for sweet release. Consciously owning up to and honouring an ending, however big or small, will help ready your heart for the road ahead.

♈ ARIES

Two ardently aerodynamic daredevils forever ready to leap from the plane, Aries and Sagittarius share a call to come at life's challenges with endless founts of optimism. Embrace a little Sagittarian faith this month, releasing any obsessive focus on beating the odds and celebrating victories that go way beyond win/lose.

✦ Jupiter is back in your sign this month and it's better than ever. Drop the agendas and clear the calendar of any constraints, as you come at the month full-throttle – expecting and indulging in an unrestrained smorgasbord of soul-fulfilling snacks.

♉ TAURUS

A pair of plus-sized pleasure-seekers who relish healthy excess, both Sagittarius and Taurus are here to pile on life's extras. Borrow some Sagittarian spirit-juice this month to add to your self-made mix, easing up on your efforts and remembering that you never have to sing for your supper to ensure that you get served.

✦ With your ruler, Venus, finishing the year in your fellow Earth sign of Capricorn, while also squaring Chiron, take stock of your heart's journey with both strength and softness, smoking out any harsh stories about being broken or in need of repair.

♊ GEMINI

The round-the-world voyage to Gemini's spin around the block, Sagittarius is here to help the gemstone kid graduate into wider mindscapes. Let December be your invitation to eat at the adult table, noticing any time you limit yourself with tall tales about needing more experience to do the job that you're already doing well.

✦ This month's Full Moon in your sign is a chance to insert yourself into all available openings. Adopt a *carpe diem* credo as you slip into conversations and situations, seize flying opportunities in mid-air and just say yes instead of maybe.

♋ CANCER

The ocean sea-salt spray and the intrepid sailor searching new land, both Cancer and Sagittarius find solid ground by first surrendering to the flow. This month, embrace some of Sagittarius' avid adventurism, letting any anxieties about the future become an exhilarating chance to pen your own answers to life's 'what ifs'.

✦ With this year's Moon cycle ending with a blowout in the signs of Gemini and Capricorn, consider how you could embrace even more of your regal rainbow, turning so-called problem parts into unexpected sources of power.

♌ LEO

Two gorgeous glow-getters who can find mythical meaning in a pile of mud, fellow Fire signs Sagittarius and Leo are here to stage acts of cinematic courage. Let December be your invitation to get even looser with your largesse, crashing the party if necessary and spreading your life force around with promiscuous pleasure.

✦ As your ruler, the Sun, trines the North Node, it's game on for connecting to your higher purpose. Don't worry too much about the shape of things – trust that the grand design is in the poetic feeling rather than the careful planning.

♍ VIRGO

Well aware of life's witchy wonders, both Sagittarius and Virgo craft their inner code from clues in the external landscape. This month, borrow some Sagittarian flames to shine a light on the impact of all that you've been taking in. Challenging yourself to express rather than repress emotions will help you live with an integrity that's both solid and spacious.

✦ With your ruler, Mercury, rolling forward almost until year's end, perform acts of alchemy everywhere you go, remembering your rightful role as a meticulous magic-maker who can draw gold out of life's metal through your mettle alone.

♎ LIBRA

Forever questing towards the castles of the good, the true and the beautiful, Sagittarius and Libra are here to lovingly lift life up where it belongs. Let Sagittarius' wild ponies give you permission to commit to your mission unequivocally this month – steadying your gaze on the horizon and heading off intrepidly in search of whatever you seek.

✦ As your ruler, Venus, ends the year in high-quality Capricorn, don't be afraid to level up with your longings. Take a pass on anything that's below the mark, and trust that nothing that's meant for you will pass you by.

♏ SCORPIO

Two soul-seekers who can mine the magic out of any life experience, both Sagittarius and Scorpio are here to follow the wild trails wherever they may lead. Let December grant you permission to get radically honest about whatever is uncovered therein, remembering that sharing a truth can build as much strength as keeping a secret.

✦ A mid-month meet-up between two of your rulers, Pluto and Lilith, asks you to unwaveringly commit to your own evolutionary force, protecting a new way of being that's blossoming just like a tender green shoot coming up out of the ground.

STAR STYLE

COLOUR: Follow the tinted trails with nomadic hues, caravan colours, swirling shades and party-ready prints. Think saffron, mustard, amethyst, scorching amber, glitter-dusted taupe, confetti patterns and saturated chromatic spectrums.

FASHION: Get ready for worldwide wildness with inspo from Rio carnival queens, circus performers and Route 66. Think headdresses, rich tapestried fabrics, balloon pants, Glam Squad sweats, handheld luggage, cowboy boots and double denim. Whatever you slip into, ensure that it's fit for leaps and bounds, and have fun with hair extensions and adjustable pieces that can be sported in multiple ways.

SCENT: December's aromas are amply spiced, road-ready and spiritually inclined. Think sandalwood, cinnamon, cloves, nag champa incense sticks, bonfires, airport duty-free perfume, and sachets and sprays tucked into travel bags.

FOOD FOR THE SOUL

Experiment with flavours from far-flung lands, hedonistically heated dishes, and snacks that can be sampled on the go. Think warm curries, stone bibimbap bowls, beef jerky, molé, ancho peppers, trail mix, s'mores and anything that gets smoked on a spit.

293

D

CHART YOUR COURSE

The cosmic queen of uncharted cartographies, December's Sagittarius energy sends us glamping past trail markers and embracing our eternal seeker. Loosen your own limits and give it up to goddess with round-the-world roams to wild and holy landscapes brimming with mysterious mojo. Think the Amazon jungle, Machu Picchu, Angkor Wat, Mumbai and Rio de Janeiro's 'Christ the Redeemer' statue. Closer to home, embrace spontaneous getaways and stage festive landscape interventions with all-access train passes, road trips, public art, parades and street parties.

ELEMENTAL EXCURSIONS

Mutable Fire-sign-ruled December playfully pushes us towards exuberant existentialism and exploratory expansion. Think trampoline workouts, weekend getaways, body-paint parties, circus classes, higher education, campfire circles, philosophy texts, cross-cultural encounters, shamanic journeys, stream-of-consciousness writing and trance-dance marathons.

PLANETARY PROMPTS

Use these magic words and journal
questions to moor you this month...

RISK:

Which parts of my life have become safe, and
where am I ready to open up to more adventure?

SEEKING:

What kind of story does my life tell, and
what have I continually chased?

EXPANSION:

If there were no limits, what would I want right now?

CO-CREATION:

Where could I take a trust fall and
experiment with letting life catch me?

WILDNESS:

How can I honour my spontaneous urges and instincts?

CONCLUSION

Y ou are forever a precious part of the shifting stars that surround you – a wise weather rod full with the divine dust that birthed your flesh and bone in the first place. You are alive and present in the saturated spice of Fire, the plush petals of Earth, the atmospheric exhale of Air and the fathomless foam of Water. A vital piece of the planets' pulsations, you are worthy of and ready for every shade and shape that this year's life on Earth could possibly contain. So go ahead: open wide, and step outside.

NOTES

INDEX

ABOUT THE AUTHOR

Bess Matassa, PhD, is a New York-based astrologer and tarot reader who serves up mystical self-inquiry with a side of play, poetry, and pop music. When not busy combing the cosmos, she can be spotted sporting hot pink lipstick while wandering deserts and tropics.

Photo credit: Caitlin Mitchell

ABOUT THE NUMINOUS

The Numinous is a 'Now Age' publishing platform from Ruby Warrington, a British writer, author and thought-leader currently located in New York City. Find us @the_numinous and at www.the-numinous.com